Deal with your Past!
Case Studies with EMDR Therapy

Esly Regina Carvalho, Ph.D.

TraumaClinic Edições

Deal with your Past!
Case Studies with EMDR Therapy

Esly Regina Carvalho, Ph.D.

Deal with your Past! *Case Studies with EMDR Therapy*

This book is part of the series
Clinical Strategies in Psychotherapy, Volume 3

Originally published in Portuguese, 2016

ISBN 13: 978-1-941727-46-1
ISBN 10: 1-941727-46-8

Revision: Judith Jone
Layout: Marcella Fialho
Cover art: Claudio Ferreira da Silva &
Éderson Luciano Santos de Oliveira

Translation into English: Esly Regina Carvalho

www.plazacounselingservices.com
esly@plazacounselingservices.com

Special thanks to all of the colleagues that allowed us to tell their stories in these pages; and to *Suellen Jacqueline Gonçalves Caldeira* who helped us with the transcriptions.

Table of Contents

Gratitude

A few weeks ago, my mother finished doing the revision of this book in Portuguese. She commented on how much she enjoyed the stories, and wished there had been more of them. I could tell she was moved by several of them. One of the cases touched her so much I wrote a note to the colleague and commented on my mother's reaction to her story.

Not everyone is aware that I learned to read and write in Portuguese at age sixteen, when my family moved back to Brazil. I grew up in Dallas and did my first ten years of schooling in English. So my mother would correct my homework - and that of my sisters – enough to where we wouldn't be totally humiliated at school by what we were writing. I knew that sometimes she would go to her bedroom and close the door after looking at our schoolwork. Many years later she confessed that she would go to her room so she could laugh herself silly at the stuff we wrote. She didn't want to embarrass us, but she couldn't contain her laughter over our mistakes.

So, when she read this manuscript in Portuguese and told me, *"Your Portuguese is much improved"*, it was an exceptional compliment. It tickled a special, deep place inside where the Portuguese alphabet lives….

Last week, my mom passed away before she saw the publication of the book in which she had invested hours of reading and correction. Now she will see the book launch from a special seat in Heaven. We miss her terribly. It will be the first time I won't receive her congratulations personally, but I know that she will continue to root for me in the midst of the cloud of witnesses.

This book is dedicated to my mom, Zilda Costa de Souza.

Thank you, Mommy.

EMDR changed my life...

First, it changed my personal life…

Back in 1995, I sought out a therapist In Colorado Springs to help me heal some old stuff that was bothering me. I don't believe in carrying around any emotional baggage if I can help it. Since I didn't have a lot of options that I could afford where I lived at the time, I made an appointment with someone on my husband's insurance plan. She was a very compassionate person, and proposed doing EMDR therapy to help me with the scenes that were bothering me. She knew that I was a psychotherapist, so she gave me articles to read up on EMDR therapy, since I had never heard of it.

I walked out of that first EMDR session so amazed with what had happened to me that I decided to seek training. I wanted to treat my own clients with it. I hoped eventually to return to Latin America and take the training with me so many more people would benefit from it. I knew something inside of me had changed forever.

I just hadn't realized that my professional life was about to change as well.

I'm one of those professionals that made a commitment early on in my career to a psychotherapeutic approach called Psychodrama and I never looked back. The first time I put my foot on a stage I said to myself, *Self, you were born to do this thing!* I didn't have a good reason to change. Sure, I read up on other approaches and kept abreast of what was happening, but I loved the results and the creativity that Psychodrama offered. But when EMDR therapy came into my life, I began to study and implement it. Everything started changing at the office: the way I thought about my patients, the constant amazement with their marked improvement, how fast things got resolved. It was truly incredible to watch, especially for a therapist as experienced as I was.

Patients came in and we set up specific therapeutic goals, many of which were reached very quickly. The results were measurable and the gains irreversible. I didn't see relapses and the changes were profound and liberating. Nowadays, that has become the rule in my practice and not the exception.

EMDR therapy represents a paradigm shift in how we approach psychotherapy. Dr. Francine Shapiro commented at a public presentation[1] that it is a form of psychotherapy with a physiological base. It can change the distress attached to traumatic memories in the neuro-networks of the brain. With modern brain scans, such as SPECT scans, PET scans, MRI, etc. it is possible to physically visualize the changes in brain activity as a result of EMDR therapy. It seems we have finally found the meeting point of the mind and the brain.

This book illustrates this new approach to psychotherapy that has so totally changed my life personally and professionally. It continues to change the lives of my patients on a daily basis. Having become an EMDR Trainer, I have the satisfaction of training other colleagues, knowing that their patients will also benefit from their training for many decades.

The stories that follow are a compendium of sessions where colleagues submitted to an EMDR session during the training process. The sessions were taped and transcribed. For that reason, we maintained the colloquial form of language. Through the case studies, a variety of issues are presented. Most of the cases were comprised of only one EMDR therapy session, although several had follow-up encounters. It is possible to see the speed of resolution when the standard

---

[1] Oral presentation at the opening of the EMDRIA (EMDR International Association) Conference in September, 2006.

protocol is used. Also illustrated is the use of other protocols taught in basic training in Brazil where all of these sessions took place.

Even though many EMDR therapists will be able to put the information to good use, the book was written with the general audience in mind so that more people can learn about the force and power for change that EMDR therapy produces in our brain, and as a result, in our behavior, emotions, sensations and life decisions. Here it is possible to see how post-traumatic stress syndrome can be avoided; the resolution of phobias that were a torment for years; how to resolve dilemmas; school experiences that left their indelible mark, and finally, how resilience can be reinforced.

It is my hope that all licensed clinicians in Brazil (where I live) and around the world can treat their clients with EMDR therapy. I would like for everyone to have an opportunity to recover from the traumas of our imperfect lives and those disastrous consequences: negligence, violence, sexual and physical abuse, depression and anxiety; relationships that have soured and could be salvaged; all of this marasmus of pain and suffering which we deal with as our daily fare

The beauty of all of this is that we are part of a greater dream: that of Francine Shapiro and EMDR therapists around the world that share the desire for a world with less suffering. This book is but a small contribution towards that end.

Esly Regina Carvalho, Ph.D.
Trainer of Trainers, EMDR Institute/EMDR Iberoamérica
Clinical Director, TraumaClinic do Brasil
www.plazacounselingservices.com

EMDR sessions in Portuguese with English subtitles are available on our YouTube channel:
https://www.youtube.com/user/emdrbrasil

We offer 2-3 day intensive EMDR therapy for those who are interested (in English, Spanish or Portuguese). Appointments: +55 61 3242 5826 in Brasilia, Brazil

If you would like to sign up to receive our newsletter about events and publications visit the following link:
https://app.e2ma.net/app2/audience/signup/1773350/1732906/?v=a

When Helping Hurts:
The Tragedy of the Fire at the Kiss Nightclub

Many people were deeply traumatized as a result of the fire that ripped through the Kiss nightclub in Santa Maria, Brazil, in January, 2013, leaving over 240 victims dead, most of them young people. The emotional trauma of such an experience affects not only the survivors and their families. Those who care for them also suffer.

Sonia, a psychologist, who helped the victims and their families, went to the gym where the bodies were to be identified by family members less than 12 hours after the tragedy occurred. During the second module of EMDR therapy training she asked for help, due to the invasive nature of her memories and images resulting from that event. Here we see an example of vicarious trauma: when the one who helps also gets traumatized.

The first session was taped two months after the fire. I treated this colleague who had done so much to aid the victims' families. The emotion was so overwhelming that Sonia began to manifest symptoms of post-traumatic stress. The second session occurred the following day. The third session was held two months later at another training event.

Two years after these sessions. Sonia continues to be free of symptoms, and is now able to care for survivors and their families.

We hope that other survivors, families and those who help people in such tragedies may benefit from EMDR's healing power. Helping can hurt, and we need to care for those who help.

First session:
Sonia (S): Do you think I get through this?
Dr. Esly Carvalho (E): We'll go slowly. You know the rules.

If you need help and don't feel that you can keep going, we'll stop. We'll be careful. Hopefully, you will feel better. Shall we start?

S: Yes.

E: Tell me what's going on.

S: It's... It's hard to talk about it. The images are very strong... so many bodies. And when we [Sonia and other psychologists] went to help, we had to be brave in order to give support to those families, mothers and fathers. The worst scenes are those of the bodies, because there were so many of them. And they were so young... and people's despair and the powerlessness. That's the issue. We are hard on ourselves for the things we weren't able to do. It's all so hard.

E: Well... The most difficult part is the images in the gym? How long after the fire did this take place?

S: I went Sunday morning. We received the news... my husband and I went for a walk that morning and our neighbor was already out and about. We'd heard the sirens from the fire trucks and the ambulances during the night, and thought it was a bad accident, but never something of this proportion. We went for a walk and the neighbor said, "Have you heard what's happened? A nightclub caught fire." We thought *many people must have died*, but we'd never imagined the size of what happened. We went back to the house and turned on the TV, and then it started. The number of dead people increased by the minute: 30, 40, 100 and... The telephone started to ring.

I have a teenage daughter. She had a friend sleeping over that night. They are only 14 years old; they would never leave the house. And my husband... all of his family is from Santa Maria. He was terrified thinking about his nephews and nieces. On the television they said they needed help. We had a prior engagement in another city.

I said I was going to help out, and my husband said, "No, you're not." He tried to stop me. I wanted to go, because they needed help over there. I couldn't stay put. I was really angry with him. I wanted to go; it was the least I could do. He told me he was going to go up the mountain. So I called my sister-in-law and said, *"Please, come over, because I'm going over there to help out."* I left my children with her. The neighbor took me there.

Watching what was going on with people on television was one thing. Being there was completely different. I arrived at 11 a.m. and the place was still closed off. There was this huge crowd, despair and chaos. We identified ourselves and they let us in. It was a sports center, where events and fairs are held. There were several pavilions. Everything was centralized in 3 pavilions. We received the families in the pavilion on the right. We formed groups. Each one had a psychologist, a social worker, a nurse, and a doctor. It was chaotic; nobody knew what to do. We were totally lost.

They finally opened the gates and the families came in. They wanted to know about their children. And we didn't know. We didn't know what to do. One never knows what to do. The helplessness. There was nothing to say. And people asked, *"Where should I go?"* I remember it well, *"Where should I go? Should I stay here? Should I go to the hospital?"* "I don't know. Stay here."

They read out the children's names. This part was terrible. People fainting and being sent to the doctors. I remember a doctor saying, *"Out here it's one thing. Inside is really bad. If you can't handle it, don't go in. It's horrible just terrible!"* We went inside, and it was a mess…

E: Let's try to organize this a little bit. This is what I'd like for us to do: I want you to run through the whole thing. What would be the starting point of this "video"? When you met your neighbor? When you arrived there at 11 a.m. Where does the worst part of the situation begin?

S: Inside.

E: Inside. At what point?

S: The moment I saw the bodies. The moment we took family members to identify the bodies.

E: And at what point does it end? When you got home? When you left the place? A few days later? Up to now?

S: Well… a week later I took a vacation. So I calmed down. I left the city. I think it ends when I left town, but now I'm back in town, and it got really hard again.

E: So, it lasted a week. Did you go back later to help out in the following days, or did you go just the first day?

S: I went back on Monday and Tuesday… and I went to some meetings, to help make decisions. I went back on Tuesday, too.

E: When you think about the impact of these images, what do you think about yourself that is negative, false and irrational?

S: That I'm incapable.

E: And if I could change all of this with a magic wand so that things were all right, what would you like to think about yourself that is positive and true?

S: That I did what I could.

E: And when you think about that scene, and the words "*I did what I could*", on a scale of 1 to 7, where 7 is completely true, and 1 is false, how true do you feel these words to be right now, when you think about that?

S: Four.

E: When you think about that difficult experience, what emotions come up for you now?

S: Helplessness, powerlessness.

E: And how much does it bother you on a scale of 1 to 10, where 10 is the maximum distress you can imagine, and 0 is nothing?

S: How much does it bother me now? I think it's a 9.

E: You know how this works. Sometimes different things may come up and sometimes they don't. Let's repeat this scene several times, so we can help you desensitize it. Run the "video" from start to finish. I'll do the movements and you let me know when you're done. You tell me when to stop. Let your brain do whatever it has to do. If you need to stop, raise your hand. You can ask me to stop anytime and we'll stop. I know this is really hard, but I hope that by doing this, you will get better, so you'll be able to do what you want, and help people if you like. OK? Any questions?

[Sonia shakes her head.}

Ok, then let's get started. I want you to think about the images, think about the words "*I am incapable*", feel this in your body, run the video, and tell me when to stop, OK?

[BLS or bilateral movements, in this case, eye movements.]

E: Take a deep breath. And now?

S: The scene of the mothers wanting to take their children home... they would say, "*Get up, wake up!*" These scenes come up real strong.

E: I'll keep doing the eye movements, but if you need to cry, may I continue the movements on your knees?

[Sonia nods in assent.] [BLS]

S: I still see it, I remember, those parents... and their anger... they were so angry... mothers crying and calling for their children. There were lots of coffins... the coffins just kept coming in... [BLS]

E: Take a deep breath.

S: Now I'm not at the pavilion anymore, where the bodies and the families are. I saw this scene where a father came for his daughters, and the son-in-law cried... people's solidarity.

There was this doctor who would give people massages, and he got very close to this one particular family. I hung around with them. They were simple folk, poor. The daughters were university students. Two sisters from a nearby town. They were poor, without any means. They didn't know which funeral home to call. We made the calls for them, my colleagues and me. We arranged for them to come... anyway, what caught my attention... now this came up... was people's solidarity... they were concerned... not with the feeling itself, but with...

I remember this guy, who lost his wife, and had to go back to identity her body. They were two sisters. The police said he had to go in, since the identities could be mistaken. He didn't want to go back, so I went back in with him. We arrived, he identified her and said, *"Look how beautiful she is,"* but they were all charred! They weren't pretty at all. There was one body... I remember thinking, *"What a horrible tattoo!"* This comes to mind a lot. Red, red... it wasn't a tattoo. He was all burnt up.

[BLS]

S: I thought... I was thinking... *"I am human"* because... I think it's hard for anyone. And suddenly, you try to find strength from somewhere, to try to help somehow... those families. One more thing... I couldn't stay any longer... I couldn't stand it... that part with the bodies. I said, *"No more."* I have my limitations. I did what I could. I stayed on the premises, walking around, listening to people, calling for doctors, looking for medicine, and taking the mothers to the bathroom. It was all we could do. This was our role. I went home at 6 p.m. When I left, my hands were red because of the gloves. I didn't even know I was allergic to them. At home, I couldn't show my kids how sad I was. No way; it was too painful. At night, I fell apart.

[BLS]

E: Take a deep breath.

S: I feel a little bit better. I am still sad, but… at least I can talk about it… without crying so much.

E: Going back to this initial experience, when you think about it now, how much does it bother you, on a scale of 0 to 10? Zero is not at all and ten is the max.

S: It's easier to look at … maybe 2.

E: What is this 2?

S: It's that body; I can't get it out of my mind. The burnt one… he asphyxiated… all the women were covered with blankets, and but not this young man… later we saw his picture in the newspaper. He caught my attention, because he had blisters all over his body. All I could think was, "*Somebody please cover him!*"

E: Go with that.

[BLS]

E: And now, when you think about it, what is the number from 0 to 10, where 10 is the maximum, and 0 is nothing.

S: I think it's nothing. I can look at it now. I can see and understand it better. I did what I could with what I had.

E: So from 0 to 10, what is it now?

S: Maximum?

E: Ten is the maximum and zero is nothing.

S: Zero.

E: When you think about this experience, the video of those scenes… You had said, "*I'm capable*", but you also said, "*I did the best I could*". You said, "*I'm human*", that everybody did the best they could, so "*I did the best I could*". Which of these expressions best describes your positive cognition now regarding that event?

S: *I did the best I could.*

E: And when you think about these words, "*I did the best I could*", think about that experience, and on a scale of 1 to 7, where 7 is completely true, and 1 is completely false, how true do you feel these words "*I did the best I could*" are, regarding that event now?

S: Five.

E: I want you to think about those scenes as a video once again, think about the words, "*I did the best I could*" and follow my fingers.

[BLS]

E: And now?

S: Well, with those conditions... I have my limitations. And it really was all I could give. There wasn't a lot more that could be done. But now, with the EMDR... I needed to become stronger. No one is ever really prepared to face a tragedy like that. It's true. It was what I could do. Give them some support, hugs, comfort, take them to the bathroom, hold their hands. There was so much solidarity. Really, there wasn't anything more I could do.

E: On a scale of 1 to 7, where 7 is completely true, and 1 is completely false, how true do you feel there words are, *"I did the best I could"* now, when you think about the accident?

S: Seven.

E: Let's strengthen it? Think about that experience, think about the words, *"I did the best I could"* and follow my fingers.

[BLS].

E: Take a deep breath. And now?

S: Better. I think about that place again and all that I did, and all the giving. Everyone gave. No matter how little, but each person gave something. And I think about how important it must have been to those families at that time, even though they were hurting so badly.

E: I want you to close your eyes, think about that difficult experience, think about the words *"I did the best I could"* and see if there is any distress in your body.

S: No. I had felt a tightness in my chest, but not now.

E: As you are aware, the reprocessing may continue after the session is over. If some of those thoughts and pictures come up, that's normal. We ran through the recent events protocol, which is what we wanted to do in this case. Of course this session isn't going to do away with all the sadness completely. You will continue to work on the grief part of it, the loss... they were really very distressing scenes. People lost their lives. But I hope that when you think about it, you won't be as distressed as when we started our session. How does that sound?

S: Yes, sounds good.

E: Think about it one more time and see how you are. [Pause] Are you OK?

S: Yes, I'm OK.

E: I would like to thank you for your generosity, for your willingness to share this experience with us. {There were EMDR students behind the one-way mirror when this was taped.] I hope you will be able to help these families somehow. Hopefully, you may be able help them again.

S: I'd like to thank *you*!

E: I believe you'll be able to contribute more when you feel better, right?

S: Yes, thank you.

E: Thank you.

(End of first session.)

The next morning:

E: How are you today?

S: I'm doing well, calmer. I had a wonderful night's sleep. I hadn't been able to sleep well for a long time. I would wake up at night for other reasons. But I slept well, with no nightmares. In fact, I remembered some of those scenes, but I could do it with serenity, with great calm. I feel good, I feel... the only thing I have is some pain in my shoulders, a really strong pain. I've massaged them to see if it gets better. I've linked it to the weight I've been carrying for over a month. It was really heavy and now that things have eased up, I'm relaxed. But I feel much better.

E: Your aspect is completely different. It looks like you are ten years younger! Really amazing the difference. When you think about the pain in your shoulders now, on a scale of 0 to 10, where 10 is the highest level of distress and 0 is nothing, how much does it bother you now?

S: It's about a four.

E: Would you like to do some eye movements to see if we can clear it up? We don't have a lot of time, but we can try it. Think about the pain, the distress in your body, and fellow my fingers. [BLS].

E: Take a deep breath.

S: It's better. I feel some tingling, but it is light and calm.

E: Zero to ten?

S: Still a two.

E: Let's continue? [BLS].

E: Take a deep breath.

S: Real calm.

12

E: Zero to ten?

S: Zero. Calm.

E. Once again, go back to that experience that we worked on yesterday. What is it like now?

S: It's calm. No negative beliefs, only positive. I know that I did what I had to do. For you to have an idea, last night my nephew who lives in another country and some family members asked me about what happened that day. I was able to talk about it without crying like crazy. Obviously, I get sad about it... it takes time to get over it. I think that's normal. But I can do that in a normal way. I was able to talk about it, and share what happened. Before the session, I couldn't even begin to talk about it. I'm really much calmer now.

E: Once again, I want to thank you for your generosity in sharing this experience with us. The difference between yesterday and today is enormous. The reprocessing continues after the session, as you well know, and it's possible that in the next few days, new things may come up. But the therapeutic gains are irreversible. We know that what you have gained thus far is yours to keep.

S: Thank you very much!

E: Thank *you*!

Two months later:

E: Sonia, tell us, how are you doing? How long has it been since our last session?

S: Two months.

E: Yes, two months. Tell me, when you think about that experience that we worked on... how is it now?

S: It is fine. I feel like it went really well. Every day, in town, I face situations that remind me of the tragedy. It is not something that can be forgotten. Last week, one more person died [from injuries sustained in the result of the fire]. The family members have been organizing themselves. The city is still in mourning.

I do not have enough words to thank you... I'm grateful from the bottom of my heart. The good you did me was enormous. I left the session that Saturday... well, that night I was able to tell the story. I can look at the scenes, and think about the incident. I remember everything that happened. Of course, feeling sad is normal, but it's OK now. I know that I did everything I could with the means I had. A month after the tragedy, I began treating a survivor of the tragedy.

E: You were able to do it?

S: Yes, of course! And it went well. I was able to do it. She has begun going out again. Something she couldn't do before. She even went to a nightclub. So for her... and for me, to have this feedback from a patient is really good. And now I've started treating someone who lost two girlfriends. Her guilt is greater than the sense of having survived it all, because they were going to go together, and in the end, she didn't go that night. *"I could have saved her"*, and the truth is, no, she couldn't have. But I am doing well. The EMDR approach is fantastic.

E: You are doing EMDR therapy with them?

S: Yes.

E: And it is going well?

S: It's going really well, and the families thank me. *"Look at what you are doing!"* It's the approach we are using. I'm doing well and I can transmit this to them.

E: That's what needed to happen, that you could get well enough so that you could choose to treat them or not. But the first thing was for you to get better. People do not always realize that watching a tragedy unfold or listening to what happened is also traumatizing. Even though you weren't at the nightclub fire, what you saw was overwhelming. just like it was for many of the doctors, nurses, support personnel and others in town. This is a small town where everybody knows everybody else. And a large number of tragic deaths, young peoples' lives cut short. The fact that you heard it all first-hand is also very significant. We were able to restore your ability to help others.

S: Yes, for sure. And there are many stories. I spoke with the mother of a young man who lost 16 friends in the fire. I told her we could try to help him. He's already in therapy, but we told him we could see him. I treated her niece and the aunt asked me, *"What did you do with her? Her parents would like to thank you." "Why don't you bring your son?"* But people resist what they don't know. But they are seeing the results in the lives of others, so I really hope this young man will come and see me.

E: I am really happy. I want to thank you once again. Even though it was only one session, we were able to work out what needed to be done with this specific situation. Now we have one more person in Santa Maria that can help others. I'm the one who should thank you for giving us the chance to do this reprocessing.

S: An important thing with those of us who are getting trained [in EMDR] is that you have to do the reprocessing in order to see the importance and the changes that occur. It is fantastic. And one can transfer this to the patient.

E: Yes, that's right, because we really believe it works. That is the most important thing. Those who help others also need to be treated. Not just the survivors, but those who help also need it.

S: Yes, that's right!

E: Thank you.

Several years later, I got in touch with Sonia again in order to ask her for permission to publish her story, and her gains were maintained. She continues to help people who were involved in the tragedy, treating them with the EMDR therapy she learned and that helped her reprocess the terrible experience that she went through as well.

It's important to remember that people who help also hurt. Helping personnel also need help. Helpers need to be treated. Vicarious trauma is a form of trauma that can leave sequela if not treated appropriately.

That Look on His Face

People tend to think that only heavy-duty traumas get in the way of life. But one of the things that have become clearer and clearer with EMDR therapy is that even apparently simple situations can leave their mark.

In the following pages we will see how present-day difficulties are linked to childhood experiences, which didn't seem to have any significant importance at all. Even adverse experiences considered the *"light"* kind can produce problems in adulthood. Perhaps that is one of the reasons that most people can benefit from EMDR therapy.

At the beginning of this session we give the initial instructions that are generally presented to our clients so they understand what EMDR therapy is all about. Then we check which bilateral movements are appropriate and which should be eliminated from the toolbox. A metaphor is explained and chosen in case it becomes necessary to slow down the processing.

T: So, Sally, ready to get started?

C: Let's do it!

T: When a trauma occurs, it seems that it gets blocked in the nervous system along with the original image of what caused it, the thoughts, motions, and feelings as well. This content can combine reality with phantasy, besides the images that symbolize the moment or feelings we have related to it. The eye movements or other bilateral movements seem to unblock the nervous system so that the brain can't process the experience. This can also happen during the Rapid Eye Movement (REM) sleep when the eye movements seem to process the unconscious material. It is important to remember that it is your brain that is in charge of healing and you control the process.

We are going to observe what's happening to you. I need for you to tell what's going on with you. Sometimes things are gong to change, and sometimes they won't. I'll ask you on a scale of zero to ten, where ten is the maximum distress you can imagine and zero is nothing, or neutral. Sometimes things will change, and sometimes they won't. There's not a "right way" of doing this, so answer as precisely as you can about what's happening to you without judging if it should be happening this way or not. Let whatever happens, happen, because your brain knows the way. We will do some bilateral movements for a bit, and then we'll talk about what's going on

If at any point you want to stop, raise your hand. (Therapist raises her hand to illustrate it) Raise your hand so that I can see that you understood. [Client raises her hand.] Great. If you are working with your eyes closed and you open your eyes, I will also understand that it is a stop sign, OK?

We will adjust our chairs into the "ships passing in the night" position and test the bilateral movements. We will see which ones work best for you. Follow my fingers and tell me the distance that is confortable for you. [Therapist raises her hand and fingers and stops about 30 inches from the client's face.]

C: Closer.

T: OK. I will move my hand closer to you very slowly and you tell me where it's good for you.

C: OK [Client asks the therapist to stop about 20 inches from her face.]

T: Is this good?

C: Yes.

T: I'm going to move my chair closer to you so that I can be in a more comfortable position for the eye movements. (Therapist sits in front and to the side of the client.

T: Let's try the horizontal movement. [Therapist does the horizontal movement.] How's that?

C: Fine.

T: Let's try the diagonal movement. [Therapist does the diagonal movement.]

C: No. I didn't like that.

T: Let's try the other diagonal, because sometimes people don't like one of the movements but like the other one. [Therapist tries the other diagonal movement.]

C: I didn't like that either.

T: Let's try the auditory movements. [Therapist does the auditory movements.]

C: No.

T: Let's try the tactile. Please place your hands on your legs. May I touch your hands?

C: Yes. [Therapist touches the back side of the client's hands alternately.]

C: Yes, that's OK.

T: May I try it on your knees?

C: Yes. [Therapist taps the bilateral movements on her knees.]

C: It's better than the tapping on my hands.

T: OK. Every once in a while a metaphor can help create some distance between the painful experience and us. For example, you can imagine you're are traveling on a train and looking out the window, and you can observe your thoughts, images feelings and sensations as if they were scenes passing by. Or you can imagine the experience as if it were a movie on the television or the movie screen. Which of these metaphors do you prefer?

C: The one of the movie screen.

T: OK. [Therapist takes note.] Do you already have a calm place?

C: Yes. It's a terrace on a building in New York. It's a garden. It has a bench, flowers, a lot of green and sunshine. There's a bit of a breeze and down below is the noisy city.

T: And what is the word that you associated to it that helps you bring it up?

C: Tranquility.

T: Tranquility. [Therapist takes note.] OK, so I would like for you to close your eyes for a moment and go to this place.

C: [Client closes her eyes.] Yes.

T: Can you feel it as being very present for you?

C: Yes.

T: OK, then let's move forward.

What is it you would like to work on today?

19

C: I have a bad feeling when someone looks at me with an angry scowl. I lost my father about five years ago, and as a result, we children inherited the business and had to run it. I have a sister who is a lot like my father. In fact, she is his spitting image. She has the same look and that has always bothered my a lot. I have a memory as a child where I short-circuited the TV and my dad wouldn't speak to me for a long while.

C: I have two memories with the same scene: my grandmother because I burned the vacuum cleaner, and my dad because I burned out the TV.

T: So, are you thinking about the scene with your dad?

C: Yes. We went to the farm for the weekend. There were more people there and he wouldn't talk to me. He would talk to other folks and ignore me. The way I remember it in my head, he bought a present for somebody who was celebrating a birthday. It was a little kitchen mixer for children. Something I really wanted. Well, he bought it for someone, for my cousin, his godchild. I felt pretty crummy about that. And my sister… when we have business meetings, she makes the same scowl as my dad, same faces. I feel like getting up and leaving. I don't want this anymore. It bothers me. It's to the point that I get a physical sensation, my chest gets tight, and it bothers me.

T: How about we start with the older memory, about your dad?

C: That's fine.

T: If you could describe a scene, a photograph, of the most difficult part about it, when you were a child, what would it be?

C: The kitchen on the farm. There were several people there. It was some party they were having that weekend. I was in the kitchen and he came in. He talked to somebody who was there and didn't even look at me. And left. I felt really bad.

T: And when you think about this scene, what do you think about yourself that is negative?

C: I think it is: *I did something wrong.* I am… something like, *I'm not that important…*

T: I'm not important.

C: Yes.

T: Can we use that expression?

C: Yes... I think there's a better one: *I'm disposable.*

T: OK.

C: I think that's better.

T: And when you think about this difficult experience, what would you like to think about yourself that is positive?

C: That I'm not disposable, that I am important.

T: *I am important*, is that OK?

C: Yes.

T: So, when you look at the scene of this experience, how true do you feel that these positive words, *I am important*, are on a scale of one to seven, where one is false and seven is completely true?

C: When I think of this scene?

T: Thinking about this scene and the words, *I am important*.

C: One

T: Totally false?

C: Yes.

T: When you bring up this experience now, with the negative words, *I am disposable*, what emotions come up for you?

C: A tightness in my chest.

T: That's more of a physical sensation.

C: You're asking for an emotion?

T: Yes.

C: Distress. It's a feeling... like an anxiety.

T: Anxiety?

C: Yes.

T: OK. On a scale of zero to ten, where ten is the greatest distress that you can imagine, and zero is none, when you think about this image, this difficult experience that you have just described, how much does it bother you now?

C: About a seven.

T: OK. You said that you had a tightness in your chest?

C: Yes, right here (raises her hand to her chest). My heart beats faster.

T: OK, then let's start the desensitization part. You already know how this works. You can stop at any time by raising your hand, the stop sign.

Go back and think about the negative words, I'm disposable, think about where you feel that in your body and follow my fingers. (BLS). Take a deep breath. Let it out. What comes up for you now?

C: I keep seeing the scene. There was a lot going on in the kitchen, people were talking and there I was.

T: Go with that. [BLS]. Take a deep breath.

C: The scene is still in the kitchen. My dad comes in and talks to people. I'm looking on, and it's as if I'm not noticed. Other scenes come up that are all mixed in with other things I've gone through... when I took two stitches on my leg because I climbed up on top of the closet. When I came down, the knob caught my leg and pierced it. I was afraid... that my parents would arrive and this would be a bother to them, all this tumult. They took me to the hospital and said, *you can't cry, because this is your own fault. If you hadn't climbed up there, none of this would have happened.*

T: Go with that. [BLS]. Take a deep breath.

C: Another scene came up of my dad at our house. He was always very serious, with an angry scowl. We knew it was him by the way he walked. The hallway floor was wooden in the house we lived in back then. So we always knew when he was walking by. And he had a big set of keys. When it was time to go to school and he was going to take us, everybody had to get into the car real fast, or he would get mad. My mom was calmer, perhaps too much so. I remember her saying that we had to behave well, because if my dad didn't like what was going on at home, he wouldn't want to stay there.

T: Go with that. [BLS]. Take a deep breath.

C: Several scenes came up, especially about my mother always telling us kids that we had to behave, be good and not fight, and not be a bother. My dad traveled a lot and when he came home, and there was fighting going on, he wouldn't want to be home. I remember how much I wanted to be able to leave home and move on with my things, live my own life.

Another scene I remembered was about a fight they had many years ago. I was little and I remember listening behind the door. My parents were arguing in the kitchen once again. My mom was boiling some milk, to prepare a baby bottle for my younger sister I think it was. They were arguing because my dad had received an anonymous letter saying that my mother was having an affaire with somebody. They fought a lot, and I was listening behind the door.

T: Go with that. [BLS]. Take a deep breath.

C: Several scenes come up about my dad. There was a problem at the school where my mother taught, and when the principal changed, several husbands got letters about their wives, who were teachers there. My dad was sullen for months. He wouldn't speak to her at home. Now that I think about it, he wouldn't speak to anyone. I remember several times hearing my mom cry in her bedroom. They had other arguments and he would just not say anything. He would spend months like this, isolated, and not talk to anyone. The climate was really heavy and tense. I remembered things like when we would come home from a party, and we would come in on tiptoe. All we had to do was walk past his door and he would open it. He would be there waiting for us, that look on his face that meant: *always the last ones to get home.*

T: Go with that. [BLS] Take a deep breath.

C: I'm thinking of all of these meals we had at the table together where we just had to sit there. Usually there was some kind of fight. There are four of us kids so we could argue when my dad was there. We had to be really quiet, because at lunchtime he had to talk to folks at the stock market in a different time zone. He worked at the stock exchange and all of this trading in a foreign country was going on at our mealtime, so we couldn't even have a conversation. At dinnertime it was the news on TV. So we had to respect the rules that were imposed on us. Since he traveled a lot, when he was home, things went one way. And when he was away, it was different. But when he was home he was always in a bad mood with the angry scowl.

T: I get it. Go with that. [BLS]

Take a deep breath.

C: I see all of us at the table in the kitchen. My dad is eating and wrapped up in his own thoughts. There's all of this silence. Everyone is quiet. We had to think twice before we said anything so we wouldn't make things worse, or so he wouldn't get in a foul mood. Depending on what we said, it could trigger something bad.

T: So, in this scene what's the problem?

C: His scowling face.

T: OK, let's go back to the original scene, the one with which we started. On a scale of zero to ten, where ten is the maximum distress that you can imagine and zero is none, how much does it bother you now?

C: Still a seven.

T: What is it in this scene that bothers you so much?

C: The indifference.

T: OK. Go with that. [BLS]

C: I think what bothers me most in these scenes, and the one with my grandmother, is that people perceive he's not talking to me.

T: Is that it? Let's go with that.[BLS]

C: That's what makes me feel bad, as if I were being excluded from the process.

T: I see. [BLS]

C: I was thinking... maybe they were just people who were always in a bad mood?! [Laughs].

T: It sure seems like it, doesn't it?

C: And I was too little to understand that. It seemed like it was about me.

T: Yes. Go with that. [BLS]

C: It's like it paralyzed me. This kind of attitude still paralyzes me and I can't move. But I thought: I could have left that place, and gone out to play.

T: Think about that.

[BLS] Take a deep breath.

C: OK, so I need to go out and play, but I can't seem to do it.

T: What is keeping you from doing that?

24

C: It's as if... [pause]

T: Yes?

C: The feeling I have is that I'm between going and staying... why don't I ask if I did something wrong?

T: Yes.

C: But then, I think I was too little to ask something like that.

T: That's true. [BLS]

C: I would worry about him, and my mom... his angry face. If we bothered him, it would be our fault. And then I remembered a fight on the beach. I was about 15 or 16 years old. I don't remember the reason for the argument, but my mother took me to the bathroom and told me she couldn't separate from my father, because her salary wasn't enough to support us. But she said that as if he wouldn't help us out! That was her story. This is a rationalization I put together later on, but I remember all of this as if it was menacing in some way.

T: Threatening...

C: But what is strongest is my sense that this could really happen. And in the end, they never did separate. But he was always in a bad mood, and I was always concerned about how things were going.

T: Sounds like there really were a lot of things that felt threatening?

C: Yes, but none of it was real, nothing concrete...

T: But when your mom says: *I can't separate from your dad*, it sounds menacing, as if there were some kind of threat, that they would split up if you didn't behave?

C: Yes, yes, that's it.

T: Go with that. [BLS]

C: [Client raises her hand as a stop signal.] This is what came up: the angry scowl mean, *something bad is going to happen*. If the person's face looks good, then it means that everything is OK.

T: Go with that. [BLS].

C: Something else came up, like this: and angry face means things aren't going well and he could go away, leave us. And then I thought, if he leaves, what could happen?

T: What could happen? [BLS]. Take a deep breath.

C: I got blocked.

T: OK, then let's go back to the original incident, the one with which we started. Now when you think about that, on a scale of zero to ten, where ten is the greatest distress that you can imagine and zero is none, how much does it bother you now?

C: About a five.

T: What is this five? What does it mean?

C: Now I see the scene like this: he comes in, talks to people. I'm there, but I don't feel like that anymore… it's not so personal.

T: It's not about me?

C: Yes, that's it.

T: Go with that. [BLS]. Take a deep breath.

C: It's his stuff, his baggage. Now when I look at the scene, I see the adults talking together, and I don't feel so left out. As if I wasn't supposed to be there anyway. That was no place for a child. I should have been outside playing. The other kids were out there, and I was just listening.

T: [BLS].

C: I see something like this: maybe it had something to do with the television. Maybe he was mad that day because of other things that had nothing to do with me, and I made the connection that he was always mad and irritated with me…

C: Yes, that's right. This was just one more thing on his list.

T: One more thing. Go with that. [BLS]

C: He really was an irritable person. So, let's leave him alone and I'm going outside. This isn't my issue, not my problem.

T: [BLS]

C: I see myself playing outside. But the picture is like this: I wonder if my mom would say that he was upset with me? Maybe she was the one who said that kind of thing? It wasn't him; it was her.

T: Let's go back to the first experience. Now when you think about that, how much does it bother you from zero to ten?

C: Hm, a one.

T: And what is this one?

C: It's like a bit of a doubt... just so I don't say it's zero. I don't know. Maybe it's gone down too fast?

T: Then track down this doubt. [BLS]

C: Yes, I see myself out of that place, that kitchen. I'm outside. It doesn't bother me anymore.

T: *It doesn't bother me*, on a scale of zero to ten means zero?

C: Yes, that's it.

T: The words, *I'm important*, are they still valid for this experience or are there other words you would like to use?

C: Yes, I think it's good.

T: OK, then when you think about this initial experience, and the words, *I am important*, on a scale of one to seven, where seven is completely true and one is completely false, how true do you feel these words are now?

C: Maybe it's not, *I am important.*

T: OK, what would it be then?

C: Maybe it's like, I can take care of my life and play. *I can take care of my life.* Not on this level of importance, but in the sense that I can quit worrying about it.

T: So what's better? *I can take care of my life,* or *I can quit worrying about it?*

C: Thinking about that situation, *I can quit worrying about it.* It's not about me.

T: Yes, that's it. It's not about you.

C: Exactly.

T: So, when you think about these words, *I can quit worrying about it,* on a scale of one to seven, where seven is completely true and one is completely false, how true do you feel these words are now?

C: Seven.

T: Think about the initial experience, Think about the words, *I can quit worrying about it,* and follow my fingers. [BLS] Take a deep breath.

C: Seven.

T: Seven?

C: Yes. It's good. [Laughs].

T: Close your eyes and concentrate on this difficult experience that we have been working on, and the words, *I can quit worrying about it,* and examine your body, and tell me if you feel an distress, or discomfort.

C: No. Everything is fine.

T: Everything is fine. Good. This reprocessing that we did today may continue after our session ends. It is possible that during the day or during the week you may have other insights, or thoughts. Other memories may come up for you, or you may dream about some of these issues. IF this happens, just take note of what is happening. You've done a really great session, but if by chance anything comes up, feel free to give me a ring. I don't think anything much is going to happen in that sense, but just in case, take note and we'll work on it in the next session.

C: Sounds good.

T: Thank you very much. See you soon.

set up.

1. Elicits scene.

2. when you think about the scene, what do you think about yourself that's negative? (false + irrational.) N.B. doesn't ask more open qⁿ neg thoughts that could cover safety eg.

3. Starting BLS Think of neg words, where do you feel them in body, start!

4. She often tracks back to original image, checks Subs what is it that makes it a 6 (eg) BLS on what client describes.

Rat Phobia

Maybe phobias and irrational fears are some of the problems that most afflict people. They come in different shapes and sizes: fears of elevators, flying in an airplane, escalators, heights, leaving home, closed places, animals – it is a really long list. The common aspect of these phobias is how they limit people's lives. No matter how hard they try, they cannot get over the fear, or when they do, it is done so with enormous effort and anguish. The person may even be able board the airplane, but they suffer during the whole flight.

The case we share in the following pages is an example of a classical situation where a previous experience causes the phobia. Perhaps people are unaware of the consequences in insisting in certain behaviors or subjecting children to. We are deeply aware that traumas – and phobias – do not get better with time, at least not spontaneously. To the contrary: the tendency is for it to get worse. Usually it will not get better without treatment. Time goes by, but the problem doesn't go away. No matter how much a person understands that the elevator is not the boogieman, the irrational (and phobic) part inside continues to believe in imminent danger. One of the most characteristic aspects of phobias is the sense of being in danger. All of the internal alarms go off, and yell: "*Danger! Danger! Danger!*"

People will also develop a phobia without remembering the cause. Often during EMDR sessions this memory is recovered in spite of the fact that it is is not the goal of EMDR therapy to recover memories. This happens often enough that we know that no one is phobic for no good reason. Something happened even if the person doesn't remember.

In some cases, when the person really can't remember the originating cause, we can suspect that something may have happened in utero, difficult births or the first years of life. The child really only begins to have cognitive memory after 24 months of age, so earlier memories tend to be highly somatic. The body remembers everything from conception, even if the mind can't do the same.

Karen is a colleague that agreed to do a taped session. She

wanted to get rid of her fear of rats. She commented that she was terrified of them. See how one EMDR session changed her life.

T: You mentioned that you are afraid of rats. What is that like for you now?

C: Now? It's a really old problem that bothers me a lot. During the university, the situation that bothered me the most was when we had to handle rats in class. We even had to open them up. I would really get upset about that. With all of the comings and goings, at one point the teacher threatened to fail me. And I said, *"No! I'll do anything, just don't put me in the same room with the rats!"* So he had to take my hand and see that I really couldn't pick up the rat.

This would also happen when I would go for a walk on the beachfront with my girlfriends. If they said, "There's a rat!" I would freeze. [Nervous laugh.] I freeze, and a bunch of things happen to me. Even if I see one on television, I feel sick. My husband made fun of me when we first started dating. He would say, "Ah, you are making this up... until the day I fainted. Then he realized it was for real. So, if I see one on television, or even hear people talk about them, I get really upset. If I just see a picture of one, I start feeling sick.

T: Do you remember the first time this happened?

C: The first time? I only remember what I think was the trigger for all of this.

T: OK, let's hear it...

C: Our family... both on my mother's as well as my father's side, were landowners. My grandfather had a farm and we would go there often. At night, we cousins, all of the children would run around and play until they said it was time to go to sleep. In the midst of all of the family gathered there, my dad went fishing once with my uncles. They arrived really late at night. It was dark, and nobody risked going out, I don't really know why. It was a wooden house, and the people arrived, and everyone was carrying on and the kids were really noisy.

All of a sudden my aunt, said, *"Ah, there's a rat, there's a rat. A rat ran by. Call one of the men to take care of it!"*

Then my dad, one of those strong Italians guys… and since I'm the first child and I should have been born a boy, spoke up: *"How come you're running around so scared?"*

And I began to get really tense.

"Uh, I don't know. It's a rat." I didn't even really know what a rat was.

He said, *"You can't be afraid."*

"Ah, but I am; I can't be afraid, but I am."

"Then you are going to lose your fear today."

Then, my mother, my aunt, and everybody else said: *"Don't do that! Don't do that!"*

"Yes, I am going to do it!" He had already had a couple of glasses of wine, I think. And he was determined.

The men picked up the rat, and killed it. And then my dad took a hold of it by its tail [Karen shows how with her fingers]. He sat me on his lap and said, *"Now you are going to lose your fear of rats. Watch."*

And then, I started to scream!! *"Yes you are gong to lose your fear! You are going to quit being afraid!"* he said.

I just wanted to get out of there. My mom wanted to take me away, but he wouldn't let her.

"She is going to stay right here," he said. It was a lot of drama.

"Look, I'm going to put it on your leg, so you can learn to not be afraid," and he put the dead rat on my leg… I just about died. I felt like… oh, just thinking about it makes my mouth tremble even now! It was horrible!

T: What is the worst part of what you are telling me?

C: About this scene? It's when my dad puts the dead rat on my leg, and I realize it is really dead.

T: And when you think about this situation, what do you think about yourself that is negative?

C: Negative? Going back a little bit… when he put the rat on my leg, I really wanted him to take it off. But I had to agree with him that I wasn't afraid. So when I said I wasn't afraid, then he said,

31

"*OK, you can go now*". So it wasn't till then that I was able to get away. He took the rat off and ended my torture. So there are two things: having to agree with my dad who was saying that I shouldn't be afraid and the impotence of not being able to do a thing and having to be strong.

T: So, is it, I have to agree, or I am powerless?

C: I think it's, *I am powerless*, because he just *had* to make me courageous, a courage that I don't really know that I should have had, but…

T: Of these two experiences, when you think about the rat on your leg, which better explains what you feel? What you think about yourself?

C: Being powerless.

T: So, it's *I am powerless*?

C: Yes, I am powerless.

T: How old were you at this time?

C: I think I might have been eight years old at this time, not more than that.

T: OK, so when you think about this difficult experience what words best describe what you would like to think about yourself that are positive?

C: Today? That I am strong and courageous, or that I can be courageous. That's better.

T: On a scale of one to seven, where seven is completely true and one is completely false, when you think about this difficult experience, how true do you feel these words are now, *I am courageous,* with regard to that experience?

C: Two. No, I'm sorry. Seven is completely true, that I am courageous?

T: Yes.

C: Ah, then it's seven.

T: Seven is, *I am courageous*, and one, *I'm not courageous*.

C: Then I think it's a one.

T: One?

C: Yes.

T: And when you think about this difficult experience, what emotions come up for you?

C: Wow! [Nervous laugh.] Everything. [Laughs]. My mouth trembles, I break out in a cold sweat. I'm totally frozen. I feel this bad and I'm not even seeing the rat here right now. It's only in my head.

T: These are the things you feel in your body. I'd like to know what are the emotions that come up. Emotions are things like: fear, shame, anxiety…

C: Fear, despair, anguish…

T: And on a scale of zero to ten where ten is the greatest distress that you can imagine and zero is none or neutral..

C: A ten. [Nervous laugh].

T: OK. This is what we are going to do. I'm going to ask you to think about this distressing experience, while you follow my fingers. I'm going to do this for a bit, and then I'll ask you to tell me what comes up for you. Sometimes things will change and sometimes they won't. Sometimes new things may come up, and then again, maybe not. There is no "right way" of doing this. Just let things happen and answer as precisely as you can about what's going on without judging if it should be happening like this or not. I'll do a few movements and then we'll talk about what's happening. Any questions?

C: No. *Starts with scene / thought / body.*

T: OK. Then I'd like for you to think about that difficult experience that you just shared.

C: My mouth starts trembling! [Nervous laugh].

T: Think about the words, *I am powerless*, feel these things in your body and follow my fingers. [Therapist starts bilateral eye movements = BLS].)

T: Take a deep breath; let it out. And now?

C: I'm so afraid! It's like it's coming back.

T: Let's keep going?! You know that you can ask me to stop whenever you need to, OK?

C: OK. [BLS].

T: Take a deep breath; let it out. And now?

33

C: It's getting better.

T: What is getting better?

C: Ah, my jaw isn't trembling so much.

T: Let's keep going? [BLS]. And now?

C: I'm calmer.

T: Ok, let's go back to the initial experience. When you think about that, on a scale of zero to ten, where ten is the greatest distress and zero is none, how much does it bother you now, when you think about that?

C: I think it's about a seven. *what is this seven?*

T: What is this seven?

C: There's a certain... a certain anguish still.

T: Go with that. [BLS]. Take a deep breath. And now?

C: The intensity is going down. I feel the anguish, but it's decreasing. The scene seems to be getting smaller, too.

T: Let's keep going?

C: Yes.

T: [BLS]. And now?

C: Better, I think it's better, much better.

T: Now on a scale of zero to ten, where ten is the greatest distress and zero is none, when you think about this experience that we are working on now, how much does it bother you now?

C: Hmm, the distress is in my body... there's a certain comfort now. With regard to the scene, when I think about it, it's a five.

T: What is this five?

C: It's having to look at the animal. I know it won't do anything to me, but it's bad to have to look at it.

T: Let's go with that. [BLS]. Take a deep breath; let it out. And now?

C: Hm, funny, the scene is getting fuzzy now when I try to think about it.

T: Let's go with that. [BLS]. Take a deep breath; I And now?

C: It's a different sensation now when I think about it. I even feel warmer; it's warmer. It's more comfortable.

T: Now, on a scale of zero to ten, where ten is the greatest distress and zero is none, how much does it bother you now, when you think about that?

C: Maybe a three.

T: What is this three?

C: Three, because whenever there's a possibility that a rat might show up, or I even see a picture of one, I keep imagining that there is a whole invasion of them. How strange... now I'm not even able to think about it, but even so... it's something that has accompanied me for a long time. This feeling of real discomfort.

T: Go with that. [BLS]. Take a deep breath; let it out. And now?

C: Now, it's really really really better. [Laughs]. I think it's a one.

T: What is this one?

C: It's the rat itself. [Laughs]. It's the aspect, strange and disgusting, it's disgusting, but I think it's just about the rat itself.

T: Let's keep going? [BLS]. Take a deep breath. And now?

C: Interesting. [Laughs] It is very comfortable, a lot more comfortable.

T: And now when you think about that experience, on a scale of zero to ten, where ten is the maximum distress and zero is none.

C: It is really interesting. It's not as clear as before, the image isn't clear, like when I was remembering it before. There was a real quick video that went by with all of the important moments where I had to argue and ask, *please please understand that I'm afraid, please understand*; and the millions of arguments and negotiations that I had to make up. Yeah, I don't need that anymore. It's as if I could say, *I don't need to negotiate anymore.*

T: Let's go with that. [BLS]. Take a deep breath. And now?

C: I'm fine.

T: Now when you go back to this difficult experience that we are working on, on a scale of zero to ten, where ten is the greatest distress and zero is none, how much does it bother you now, when you think about that?

C: Now? Nothing.

T: Ok. When we started you said you wanted to think, *I am courageous*. Are these words still valid for you or do you want to install something more appropriate? Think about this difficult experience.

C: I think it's, *I'm courageous*.

T: Ok. Then think about this difficult experience; think about the words, *I am courageous*, on a scale of one to seven, where seven is completely true and one is completely false, how true do you feel these words, *I am courageous*, are now, when you think about that?

C: About a six

T: What is this six?

C: This six is a bit of doubt. [Laughs]. Will I really be able to do this? [Laughs]? My in-laws have a house in a rural area, and I always go there, and I have to keep watching out to see if there is a rat. Can you imagine? They are super clean people, the house is spic and span, but I'm always on the lookout. So it's the doubt.

T: Ok, then, think about difficult experience, think about the words, *I am courageous*, and follow my fingers. [BLS] Take a deep breath. And now?

C: Excuse me. I want to take my sweater off. I'm getting hot now. [Laughs]. Wow, this is just fantastic!

T: Now when you think about that experience and you think about the words, *I am courageous*, from one to seven, seven is completely true and one is completely false, how true do you feel these words are now regarding all of that?

C: Now it is really a seven.

T: Let's strengthen this so that you can take a powerful seven home?

C: Yeah! I need to be sure! [Laughs].

T: Let's go. [BLS]. And now?

C: Now, I'm hot.

T: You defrosted? [Therapist smiles.]

C: Now I literally defrosted. I'm not frozen anymore.

T: So, on a scale of one to seven, where seven is completely true and one is completely false, when you think about that experience, and you think about the words, *I am courageous*, how is it now?

C: Now it is really strong. Seven.

T: Now I want you to concentrate on that difficult experience and scan your body, thinking on those positive words, *I am courageous*. Examine your whole body and tell me if there is any distress?

C: It's my heart now. I don't know if it's just hot, or if my heart is beating faster, because it's usually here at the base of my head (points with her hand).

T: Think about that. [BLS]. Take a deep breath.

C: Everything OK.

T: Scan your body while you think about that initial experience. Think about the positive words, *I am courageous*, and see if there is any disturbance in your body.

C: No.

T: From zero to ten, where ten is the greatest distress and zero is none?

Asks client to imagine threat scene, post processing. How well do they do?

C: Zero.

T: Before finishing our session, I would like to make you a little proposal. [Both laugh]. I would like for you to imagine going to your in-laws' farm, to see how courageous you are in that situation. Look at it as if it were a video. Imagine you are there on the farm, and think about the words, *I am courageous*, and let's see what happens. [BLS]. Take a deep breath. *Add: I can face this.*

C: I'm fine.

T: Will you be able to do it?

C: Yes, Things are really different now.

T: When you think about doing that, and you think about the words, *I am courageous, I can face this*, on a scale of one to seven, seven is completely true and one is false.

C: Seven. I can face this! [Laughs].

T: Karen, the reprocessing that we did today may continue after the session is over. It may be that during the day or the rest of the week you may have insights, thoughts, memories or even dreams. If this happens, just pay attention to what is coming up for

N.B. she only focuses on the phobia + doesn't look at the relationship with cl! father. Client volunteers that rel with father has lost its anger since the treatment.

you, what you feel, what you see and perceive, and pay attention to the triggers. If you can buy a little notebook, and write down what you perceive, your dreams, insights and new memories so that we can work on them in our next session. If you feel a need for it, feel free to get in touch with me, ok?

So, how are you now?

C: I'm good. I'm feeling, well, feeling normal, because the feeling I had before was that I wasn't normal. I was different from everybody else. Nobody else has these feelings. But not now. I'm not in a panic over it anymore.

T: I would like to thank you for sharing these experiences with us, which now allows us to become part of this story. I hope that you can really take this home and live a more normal life.

C: Normal. That's good. Thank you.

Some years later, when I contacted Karen to ask her for permission to write her session up for this book, I asked her how things had gone. She wrote back:

Well, as you know, I lived my fear of rats from the age of 12. I was always thinking that a rat could come out of anywhere at any time. I would freeze if I even saw one on the television or worse, in real life.

The physical symptoms are the ones that demonstrate how much better I am now. In fact, everything is different! Now I can watch TV and see a report about rats, on an ad, or movie. Before, I would have frozen up just from seeing it there. Now I feel free of those thoughts, and I feel good. Now I'm not worried if a rat is going to show up close to where I am sitting. I had these coping strategies, where I would run away, flee, in case something happened. And what's most interesting is that all of that was tied in with my dad. Today I can be gentle with him without that sense of being hurt or angry that I used to have when I saw him.

I just want to thank you very much for having had the opportunity to heal something that had limited my emotions so much. I even got pregnant soon afterwards! Now my daughter is two, beautiful, healthy, and super courageous! I must have influenced her!

Finding the Touchstone Event

One of the things we learn during EMDR therapy training is that today's symptoms are usually indicative of an earlier causal experience, oftentimes in childhood. In order to gain time, we try to work on the earliest event possible that is linked to the presenting problem. In a sense, it is a short cut in the attempt to solve the symptom.

In this session, Sylvania presented with an event from early childhood, but during the reprocessing phase, an even earlier memory came up, that we worked on the following day. It is possible to see how we can work in a focused way with old memories and take up the reprocessing in subsequent sessions. It also illustrates how old anxiety issues can be linked to early experiences of feeling in danger. In this case, the danger was real: there really was a chance of a child kidnapping.

It is important to remember that traumatic memories are filed away in a different way than normal memory. There is a richness of detail with traumatic memories that are not often present in those that were filed away functionally.

We also see the importance and the difficulty in getting the Negative Cognition right, that "little lie" that we believe about ourselves after difficult or traumatic experiences. Sometimes it is necessary for the therapist to offer a few suggestions in order to see wherein lay the patient's difficulty.

We can see how other issues of greater complexity came up during this session, and how they were purposefully set aside for future sessions. This client had been in psychoanalysis for a long time and came to this training from that perspective and her observations during processing are a result of her analytical therapy.

First session
C: I think I must have been four or five years old. I was in kindergarten. I was there with a colleague, a little boy. We were just playing together nicely. We had a little bowl, like a margarine cup

and inside there was a bunch of sand. Out of the blue, he picked it up and threw it in my face. It fell into my eyes and I couldn't see. There was sand in my eyes and I couldn't see. Can you imagine a speck of sand in your eye? Well, I had this huge quantity in my eyes. I can't remember exactly what happened after this, I just remember my mother coming to get me at school, carrying me home, and trying to see and not being able to do it. I had to keep my eyes closed. It really hurt, just terrible.

T: When you think about this experience that we are going to work on today, what's the picture or photograph that comes up for you regarding the moment that you would like for us to start?

C: The moment he throws sand in my eyes.

T: Ok. When you think about this difficult experience, what negative and false words best describe what you think about yourself now?

C: Ah, that I was betrayed. It's this feeling... here we were just playing. Everything was going well. And then out of nowhere he throws that stuff in my face.

T: So what would you say about someone who has been betrayed?

C: That she was the victim of the situation. It's a horribly humiliating feeling.

T: So is that the feeling? Humiliation?

C: Yes.

T: And what could we say about this child who suffered this betrayal? *I'm vulnerable? I'm exposed? I can't trust anyone? I can't see?*

C: Hm, it's a feeling like... rejection, something like that. I didn't want you to be here. I was just talking and playing with him and he threw that stuff at me. It's like, *I don't want you to be here, so disappear. Go away.*

T: As if he had said that to you?

C: I feel like that was his attitude. I interpret it that way.

T: What would there have been about you, from his perspective that would lead him to do something like that? *I'm no good? I'm not important? I have no value?*

C: I think it would be, *I am inadequate.*

40

T: OK. When you think about this experience, what would you like to think about yourself now that is positive regarding this experience?

C: What comes up is, *I'm capable.* I would pick him up by his hair, today if I could! [Laughs].

T: You bet! [Laughs]. *I am capable.* Another positive cognition that occurred to me – but you know best – is, *I'm OK the way I am.* Which do you prefer?

C: I'm OK the way I am.

T: And when you think about this difficult experience, on a scale of one to seven, seven is completely true and one is completely false, how true do you feel these positive words are, *I'm OK the way I am,* now? Thinking about that experience.

C: Five.

T: Five. [Therapist has been taking note of her replies.] And when you think about this experience and the negative words, *I am inadequate,* what emotions come up for you now?

C: I think this triggered a lot of anger, because I was powerless at the time, and I'm mad at that guy to this day.

T: When you think about this difficult experience how much does it bother you now, on a scale of zero to ten, where ten is the greatest distress that you can imagine and zero is none?

C: Sincerely? I think it's a two.

T: Where do you feel this distress in your body?

C: Here [client points to her jaw].

T: OK. This is what we are going to do. I'm going to ask you to keep these distressful thoughts in your mind while I ask you to follow my fingers. I'm going to do this for a bit, and then I'll stop and ask you to tell me what comes up for you. Sometimes things will change, and sometimes they won't. There is not a "right way" of doing this, so answer me as precisely as possible about what is going on, without judging if it should be like this or not. Let whatever happens, happen. I'll do a few movements, and then we'll talk about it. Any questions?

C: No.

T: Remember that you can always use the stop sign. Or if you want me to go faster or slower, you can ask me that as well, ok?

So, go back and think about that picture of this experience, Think about the negative words, *I am inadequate*, see where you feel that in your body and follow the movements. [BLS]. Take a deep breath. And now?

C: I don't feel anything.

T: OK. Nothing is how much from zero to ten?

C: Well, my feelings changed. Can I explain?

T: Sure.

C: It's a one. It began like this: there was a feeling in my chest. *Why did you do this to me? Why did you betray me? I hadn't done anything to you,* you know, victim stuff. Then, after a few moments, very quickly, some other thoughts came up. Not that I forgot that moment, but I think that he felt really bad about what he had done. His nickname nowadays is MarcoLoco. I don't think he's got it all together in his head. I felt sorry for him, to tell you the truth. When I see him today, I feel compassion for him.

T: And when you look at little Sylvania, who is four or five years old, and you see what happened to her, what do you perceive? Think about that for a few moments. [BLS]. Take a deep breath. And now?

C: Once again I felt like, poor little thing. *Look at what happened to you.* But then I started thinking: we are always going to have problems, but we need to keep what we learn from it. I can deal with this. I have my support system, and at that time I had my parents, and besides, bad things go away. They don't last forever.

T: Ok.

C: But all of this happened really fast.

T: And when you think about that little girl that spent two weeks without being able to see right? Think about it for a few moments. [BLS]. Take a deep breath.

C: I'm going to tell you two things that happened; one before and one afterwards. This association process is really interesting… Now that time, it was as if the sky closed up, like a stormy day. It was awful, like an operation I once had. I had the feeling that it was going to come out all right. I wanted to talk to the doctor, but they put me under anesthesia before I could do that. And when I woke up, something really had gone wrong. But it passed. I don't have that horrible feeling anymore. So what I see is that things happen and then they pass. All that tumult, the anguish, it ends. It is interesting because I would never have made that association.

I remembered something else that happened when I was three years old. I got lost from my dad on the beach. My dad was with my sister and me. I cried, cried and cried, and the lifeguard found me. He saw that there was a couple that wanted to take me with them. But he didn't let them take me. I had the feeling that if the guard had let them take me, something bad would happen. He saw that I didn't recognize them, and that I was afraid, and said, *nope, she only goes with someone she recognizes.* Then my father came and I hugged him. I remember his hair. He had curly hair, like they used at the beginning of the '80's. I was very little. I remember his big hairdo, and looking at him, and hugging him. I even remember the clothes he was wearing. I don't remember what they said I did. I could never imagine associating this scene with the other.

T: Go with that. [BLS]. Take a deep breath. And now?

C: I think everything is all right. All of a sudden, I think I must have associated it with the other scene, not the feelings, but those two moments, the sand and the sense of being abandoned... it must have been something like, *my God, why? Why here? Why with me?* I don't know, it was some feeling of betrayal. Nobody saw it. Nobody helped me. But everything turned out all right. I think it was there, and something triggered it, the experience with the sand. The image came to me so clearly. And the experiences linked together.

T: Think about that. [BLS]. Take a deep breath. And now?

C: I'm fine. Now I only have the sense of betrayal, of abandonment. I don't have to worry about things before they happen.

T: Think about that. (MLBs) Take a s from zero to ten, where ten is the maximum distress and zero is none?

C: Zero.

T: And when you think about this other situation about the little boy that threw sand in your face, on a scale of zero to ten, where ten is the maximum distress and zero is none, how much does it bother you now?

C: One

T: What is this one?

C: Today I look at him and I'm not mad at him. I feel compassion for him. But the little girl, that little child, I still feel like, poor thing. [Laughs] She's still here.

T: Go with that. [BLS]. Take a deep breath. And now?

C: I think it's better. Those conversations I had on the inside helped a lot.

T: OK.

C: I don't know if I should make an observation about this kind of treatment here [this was an EMDR training event] or if I should stay in my role as a patient. But the association process of EMDR is incredible! How one thing is connected to the other. I could stay here all day; remembering one thing, and then another, things that I had never associated, put together, but that has everything to do with the emotional logic.

T: How interesting! Now when you think about that difficult experience with that little boy, how much does it bother you now? From zero to ten, where ten is the maximum and zero is none?

C: Well, there you have it. That's the problem with not being able to stop the associative chain. That little girl remembered one thing, then another, and all of these things are in a network. But if I think about the basic issue that was bothering me, and think about how my anger got triggered every time I saw that little boy… Now there's nothing left.

T: OK. There was a moment when you said, *I would like to pick him up by his hair.*

C: No, I don't feel like doing that anymore.

T: Gone?

C: Yes.

T: Ok. From zero to ten, how much is the disturbance? Zero is none; ten is the maximum.

C: Nothing.

T: So think about this for a few more moments. [BLS]. Take a deep breath. And now?

C: [Nods.]

T: Everything OK?

C: Yes.

T: OK, when you think about that difficult experience with which we started, and think about the positive words, *I am capable*, are these the words that you still want to reinforce or are there other expressions that are more appropriate

C: What came up was, *I'm good the way I am.*

T: *I'm good the way I am?*

C: Yes. That's it.

T: OK. So, think about this initial experience and think about the words, *I'm good the way I am*, and on a scale of one to seven, where seven is completely true and one is completely false, how true do you feel these words are now for you?

C: Seven.

T: Bring to mind the difficult experience, think about the words, *I'm good the way I am* and follow my fingers. [BLS]. Take a deep breath. And now?

C: What I thought was: *Sylvania, why do you need to be on the defense when you are in front of other people?* And I answered myself: *ah, because it was something unexpected.* So, then I thought: *quit that, girlfriend. It was something that happened. How many times have you come close to other people and everything worked out fine?* And I answered: *Yes, of course.* And then: *So forget it! It's in the past; it's not part of your life in the present.*

T: OK. [BLS]. Take a deep breath. And now?

C: Nothing.

T: So, on a scale of one to seven, seven is completely true, one is false; when you think about this experience and think about words, *I'm good the way I am?*

C: I'm good the way I am.

45

T: Seven?

C: Yes.

T: OK. No distress?

C: [Shakes her head as a no.]

T: Close your eyes, think about that difficult experience that we have just worked on, think about the words, *I'm good the way I am*, and mentally scan your body and tell me if there is any distress.

C: Maybe just a little bit.

T: So think about this discomfort and follow the movements. [BLS]. And now?

C: I'm fine.

T: When you think about this discomfort in your body now, from zero to ten, where ten is the maximum distress and zero is none, how much distress do you feel in your body now?

C: Zero.

T: OK. Sylvania the reprocessing that we did today may continue after the session. It may be that during the week you may have insights, thoughts, memories or even dreams. If this happens, just pay attention to what is coming up for you, what you see, feel, think, and try to identify the triggers. Take note of things that happen during the week, such as the thoughts, the sensations, memories and experiences, and we can perhaps work on them in the next sessions. If something happens, feel free to get in touch with me. Otherwise, I'll see you next week. Anything else you would like to say?

C: I think this experience is fantastic. The associative possibility of things that I never imagined were connected is amazing. I've done years of therapy, from an analytical perspective, and never had results like these, seeing how one thing is linked to another. Obviously, I didn't tell you everything or we would be here for hours, but I think it is absolutely incredible how this processing is so fast, and its linking power. It's been possible to spend years and never understand what's bothering you; and here, we made the associative link so quickly!

T: Really neat! I'm so glad. It's interesting how you describe this with so much clarity, because that is what really happens. So let's how things develop, and how you do. I would like to thank you for sharing your experience with us.

C: Thank you.

Second Session

C: Well, like I said yesterday, because I thought I had to stay focused on that scene... but then the reprocessing started on a scene with my mother where I was playing with some friends. The mother of one of the kids wasn't real normal. She was a neighbor and had made a toy for us. I went home running and crying and my mom hugged me. She stayed there with me, but I was angry because I wanted her to go and slap the neighbor. I think that scene triggered another process that has to do with anger. I think that's the emotion that is connected to it all.

T: OK. Now when you think about that experience we worked on yesterday, that scene when you were five, how is it?

C: It's fine.

T: What does "fine" mean?

C: It's like a memory that doesn't cause me any more emotion. Yesterday, I tried several times to think about that little boy and what he had done to see what I felt. Before, no matter how little he was, I always wound up angry and thinking, I should have pulled his hair. But not now.

T: So now, when you think about that scene, on a scale of zero to ten, where ten is the greatest distress that you can imagine and zero is none, how much does it bother you?

C: Zero.

T: And you remember that other scene that came up, when you were three years old, and got lost?

C: Yes.

T: What's that like now?

C: That scene, if I think about it now, it doesn't make me angry, but I feel fear and sadness.

T: And on a scale of zero to ten, how much does it bother you now?

C: One.

T: What does this one mean?

C: I think that even though everything turned out all right, I was afraid that something could have gone wrong, that the lifeguard was going to let me go with that couple.

T: I understand.

C: That he might not protect me, because I didn't want to go with that couple. I didn't know them. So I think I still have some of that fear of what could have happened to me if he had let me go with them.

T: So, when you think about this image of that couple, and the lifeguard at your side, protecting you, what do you think about yourself that is negative? *I'm in danger? I'm vulnerable? Lost?*

C: Hmm, *I'm lost.*

T: Lost.

C: Yes.

T: And what would you like to think that is positive?

C: *I'm safe.*

T: And when you think about that scene, and think about the words, *I am safe,* on a scale of one to seven, seven is completely true and one is completely false, how true do you feel these words are now?

C: Five.

T: And when you think about that picture, and think about the words, *I'm lost,* what emotions come up for you?

C: I was very little, but I was thinking, I don't know them. They are going to take me and I will never see my father again.

T: You mentioned feeling sadness and fear. We're looking for the emotions. Do you think it could be these?

C: Yes, exactly.

T: And when you think about this, on a scale of zero to ten, where ten is the greatest distress and zero is none, how much does it bother you now when you think about that?

C: It gives me a bit of anxiety. Now that I think about it, I think it's more anxiety than I realized before.

T: How much would you say?

C: Eight.

T: And where you feel this in your body?

C: Here (places her hand on her tummy).

T: Let's work on this a little bit and see if we can get it to feel better.

C: OK.

T: So, think about the scene with the couple that you described, think about the words, *I am lost*, feel it in your body and follow the movements. [BLS]. Take a deep breath. And now?

C: It was more difficult to do today than yesterday, to bring up the memory, but the difference is that I did something I think I could have done. I kept waiting for the Lifeguard's reaction, what he was going to decide. He said, *I'm not going to let you go*. It was his decision, but I could have said, *I don't know them. Please don't let me go with people I don't know. I want to wait for my father.*

T: Think about that. [BLS]. Take a deep breath, and now?

C: Once again, it took a while. If I compare it to yesterday's session, it's more difficult today

T: More difficult?

C: More difficult for me to concentrate. I was trying to bring up the memory, but it took a while. Then I began to feel the silence, a good silence, something to enjoy, not distressful. But only at the end of the set did I remember the best scene, which is when my father found me.

T: Think about that for a moment. [BLS]

C: For a while, I was just a little happy. I remember his swimsuit, and those sunglasses people used in the 80's. And then I looked, and I wanted to jump! Now I feel the complete joy! Laughs]. I wanted to have jumped and run to get to him before he even got to me. My dad was scared, too; I mean really upset, you could tell. Now I can see his face, the relief. He was really upset.

T: [BLS]. Take a deep breath? And now?

C: I'm good. What I thought was, I could have been angry at my dad, but I wasn't. I was just happy! I don't remember getting angry. I felt, terror, fear, that kind of thing, but not anger. He was the one taking care of me; not my mom, with whom he was already having some problems. I started thinking about all of this. I hadn't realized it before. I could have been angry at him but I wasn't. There were situations where I was angry with my mom, but not with him.

T: Let's leave that issue aside to work on another day?

C: Yes.

T: Because mother issues have long roots! [Both laugh].

C: Yes, of course.

T: Our time today is shorter since this is just a follow-up session. So let's put that aside for now and you can work on it in the future. Now I want you to go back to that initial experience we were working on today. Is anything different? What's it like now?

C: I'm better because now I feel like I didn't stay passive in the situation. What bothered me was that I hadn't said I didn't want to go with them. I was waiting for his reaction, but I knew that I was in a lot of danger. I didn't need that short span of time while he was making up his mind. He was very prudent, but my attitude was – even though I was just three years old – if I said, *I don't want to go with them because I don't know them. I'm only going to go with my dad.* I mean somebody else who didn't have such good sense could have let me go with that couple. But they would have listened to me even though I was only three years old. I could have defended myself, right? So I have a sense of relief. I said it. I said what needed to be said. I didn't need to stay with that sense of danger. I only needed to speak up. Now I can say, *please God, help me! Don't let them take me!* What a relief!

T: And when you think about that scene now, on a scale of zero to ten, where ten is the greatest distress and zero is none, how much distress do you feel when you think about that now?

C: It's fine. It seems like the image got inverted. Instead of thinking more about that couple that I can still remember very clearly: she was taller and he was shorter... Now the greatest memory is of my dad hugging me.

T: From zero to ten?

C: I'd say a one.

T: What is this one?

C: It's more the sensation. When I went to say, "everything is OK" I felt like a bit of anxiety here [puts her hand on her chest].

T: Go with that. [BLS]. Take a deep breath. And now?

C: I was feeling the anxiety of waiting for my dad.

T: I understand.

C: Anxiety. I still feel it when I talk to you. Anxiety, *go away, go away, go away!* And I try to talk and calm myself down. Things are going to turn out well. Thinking the adult things, but the child said, *Oh, my God, this has to end, somebody has to come and get me soon.* That was the anxiety that I was still feeling.

T: OK, let's go with that. [BLS]. Take a deep breath. And now?

C: I exchanged the bad anxiety for good anxiety. Bad anxiety is that one where I was thinking, [my father] *doesn't come, doesn't come, doesn't come.* I exchanged it for the good anxiety because I could see him already. What I said before, that I wanted to jump into his arms, so he could hug me. That anxiety is a good thing a good thing that I have to learn to control. He's already coming, so I made the exchange.

T: [BLS]. Take a deep breath. And now?

C: I finished it with a sense of relief.

T: Now when you think about that scene, on a scale of zero to ten, where ten is the greatest distress that you can imagine and zero is none, what's it like now?

C: None. It's zero.

T: Zero. OK. So, when we started the session, you said the positive words that you would like to connect would be, *I'm safe.* Are these still the words that you want to install or did something change?

C: Yes, those are the right words.

T: So, I would like for you to think about that difficult experience that we have been working on, think about the positive words, *I'm safe,* and follow the movements. [BLS]. Take a deep breath. And now?

C: It's funny, because I've been working on this issue about anger, and another scene came up. But then I thought, Here I go again! I'm already getting angry about it. So I said that there are certain occasions that we really need to respond in anger. What that couple was trying to do was take me away. So I turned and the little girl said, *You're not going to take me! Who do you think you are?!* I laughed, because I saw myself as really little and telling these people off, telling them to go away. *Go away! Go away!* And there I stood, stomping on the ground with my little foot. They turned and went away. I didn't even need the Lifeguard. I sent them away myself! Now everything is OK.

T: Great! So, now when you think about that experience and think about words, *I am safe*, on a scale of one to seven, seven is completely true and one is completely false, how true do you feel these words are now?

C: Close to six.

T: What is this 6?

C: It's because I'm not sure they won't come back.

T: Go with that. [BLS].

C: Stop. [Therapist immediately stops the movements.] Now it's like everything else in life.

T: Ok.

C: [Laughs] Now I know what that dream I had yesterday might have been about. I wanted to go with those folks, but I said we weren't supposed to work on the dream. There was a man that was twice my size. I was little, maybe a little bigger than when I was three years old, but he would hug me, and hug me and hug me... but then, he hugged with such force that it began to break my bones. He got a broomstick and stuck it here between my ribs. He would tell me to bend over, and the broomstick would go inside of me. I think it was the phantasy that I created about what would have happened to me if I had gone with that couple. That's what I think. I never – and I need to say this here – I never ever made this association, never! It was something that just happened right now, when I said, *I have the feeling that they can't come back.* I think this fear that I had that they would return became this dream, it transformed into the dream. I don't have this dream anymore, but I think that's what it was, this fear that if they came back, that's what they would do to me.

T: Let's go with that [BLS]. Take a deep breath. And now?

52

C: I said all sorts of four-letter words to them. I think that in adult life I would have done something to them. I would make sure they wound up in jail! [Laughs].

T: For attempted kidnapping.

C: It was really interesting. I've had this dream repeated times. It's been a few years since I've had it, but it used to be very frequent, and caused me enormous anguish. That pain, that pain, that pain… and sometimes I couldn't wake up fast enough.

T: I understand.

C: I think it was my brain that took me to that association.

T: Go with that. {[BLS})

C: I don't know if it is like that. I try to produce something before I start looking at your fingers. I'm always getting good things. What I did was this: not think about that tight hug, that was breaking my bones, that could have been that bad hug, from that father, from that couple, the one that wanted to take me… that's really good.

T: Very well. Now when you think about that experience, and think about words, *I'm safe*, on a scale of one to seven, seven is completely true and one is false, how true do you feel these words are now?

C: Almost, but I still can't say it's a seven.

T: What's missing?

C: I need to keep my father's hug; keep it or substitute it.

T: Can I put my two bits in? You keep saying that you were afraid that they would come back, but I thought, what if they came back, and your father had already found you? [BLS].

C: Yes. Now it seems like everything is mixed together, but it's like this: the bad scenes are a phantasy that I made up, but that now has two images: when they were there, I wasn't there anymore. I was in my father's lap, saying goodbye to them, real cynically! [Laughs].

T: Great! Now on a scale of one to seven, where seven is completely true and one is false, how true do you feel these words are now, *I'm safe?*

C: For that scene?

T: For that scene.

C: Seven.

T: Seven. Let's do it one more time so we have a powerful seven?

C: Yes. [BLS].

T: Great! And now?

C: I'm going to share everything, OK?

T: OK. [Laughs].

C: Now at the end, other things started to come up. I'm afraid that my father might die. The words, *I'm safe*, begin to trigger other things. If he dies, I won't be so safe anymore. Another therapist told me, *My goodness, it's been twenty years that your dad is alive and still hasn't died; must be a really strong father, eh?*

And there are other things. Well, I'm safe in that scene, but if I can't hug my dad anymore…. Then other things come up. But for that scene, it's OK.

T: We'll let you work on these other things in your other therapy, because I really think those are more complex issues. When you think about this experience now, is it a seven? Is everything all right?

C: Yes.

T: Close your eyes just for a moment, and do a scan of your body. When you think about that scene, and think about the positive words, *I'm safe,* see if there is any distress.

C: No, because my safe place is right on the beach, where I got lost. I'm good.

T: Ok, Sylvania, as you well know the reprocessing may continue after the session; as you have just seen, things may continue reprocessing. Some new things may come up, so just take note, and bring it to the next session. Once again I want to thank you for your generosity in letting us see a bit of what happens inside of your head, in your brain, and how this reprocessing works. Thank you.

C: Thank you.

Dilemma:
Which apartment do I choose?

T: So, Sara, I'd like for you to tell me a little bit about your dilemma and what are your options?

C: My fiancé and I bought an apartment. At the time we had to make a quick decision so that we could take advantage of a special offer the construction company was promoting, where we got ten thousand dollars off the base price. We didn't have time to study the issue of where the sun comes from, so we bought an apartment with three bedrooms and then realized that it was not in the ideal sun position. Now we see that there is an apartment for sale with two bedrooms in an excellent sun position, but we have to pay five thousand dollars extra so that the apartment can be renovated and changed to three bedrooms.

T: So, the two-bedroom apartment can be transformed into three bedrooms, but you have to pay five thousand dollars?

C: Five thousand dollars.

T: OK, so that we can give these options a name, can we call it the two-bedroom option or the three-bedroom option? How does that sound?

C: Yes.

T: With the two bedroom option you have to pay five thousand dollars to turn it into three bedrooms, but it has sunlight the way you want it, and the other one that you have already bought is all ready, three bedrooms, but the sun isn't in the right position.

C: Right.

T: OK. I would like for you to choose one hand where you can imagine placing one apartment option inside, and the other hand will have the other option. So tell me which is which.

C: In the right hand is the two-bedroom option and in the left is the three-bedroom one.

T: So in the left hand is the apartment to which you are already committed.

C: Yes. It is ours. We are committed, but the two-bedroom one is on reserve and we have to define by Tuesday which one we are going to keep.

T: Tuesday... so you kinda need to leave here today with this resolved...?

C: Right! [Laughs].

T: So, I would like for you to imagine that you are putting the three-bedroom option in your left hand.

C: May I close my eyes while I do this?

T: Yes, of course. And place the other option in the right hand.

C: OK.

T: And when both options are real clear, close your hands, and hold on to the options you have.

C: Ok.

T: So, I am going to start a bit of processing. You know how this works, and then we will comment. If you need to stop at any point, you can always do so. If you feel overwhelmed at any point, please feel free to ask me to stop. OK?

C: OK.

T: So, let's start with a few movements and see how things unfold. Think about both possibilities.

C: And I keep my hands like this? [She has both hands closed in her lap.]

T: Yes. If things change, that's fine, but let's start this way. [Therapist has already set up the images, cognitions, emotions and sensations for each hand.] Think about both options, think about the negative words for each one, see where you feel this in your body, and follow the movements. [BLS – eye movements]. Take a deep breath. What comes up for you?

C: The apartment with two bedrooms, the view is better; it is really beautiful. The sun comes up from the mountains, and I have a full range view. The one with three bedrooms isn't so perfect.

T: OK. Let's continue. [BLS]. Take a deep breath. And now?

C: Here comes my mother into this issue! [Laughs].

T: Your mom turned up?

56

C: Yes, because the apartment isn't as perfect as we had imagined it to be. And we plan to stay there for the rest of our lives. It's the beginning of our lives together. And my mother's phrase comes up: *it's not good to invest in something that you aren't going to stay in for the rest of your lives, that isn't the place you had idealized, or isn't in the area of town you want to live in.* Five thousand dollars. I know it is weighing on me, because of my mother's words.

T: Go with that. [BLS]. Take a deep breath.

C: The issue is: am I willing to pay an extra five thousand dollars for a better view? [Laughs].

T: OK. Let's go with that? [BLS]. And now?

C: Well, paying five thousand dollars for a better view is five thousand dollars! [Laughs]. But the view is more beautiful [Laughs].

T: Do you have any idea how long you intend to live in it?

C: Oh, maybe three years.

T: Go with that. [BLS]. Take a deep breath.

C: I blame myself for having chosen an apartment with three bedrooms without having looked at the issue of the sunshine, especially when you think about where we live and it's really cold.

T: Go with that. [BLS]. Take a deep breath.

C: Here comes my mother again: *how come you didn't see this before? For Pete's sake! What irresponsibility and you want to get married?!* [Laughs].

T: Let's go with that?

C: Yes. [BLS].

T: Take a deep breath. And now?

C: Now I realize that from the very beginning I liked the two-bedroom better, precisely because of the view and the sunshine. The three-bedroom was more logical, but the one I really liked was the two-bedroom one. I let it go because it only had two bedrooms.

T: When you made your choice, did you know you could transform the two-bedroom apartment into three bedrooms?

C: No, I didn't know that.

T: Let's continue.

C: Yes.

T: [BLS]. Take a deep breath.

C: Something that went through my head is that if I had known of the possibility of transforming the two into a three-bedroom apartment, I would have probably signed the contract for it because it really was the one I liked better.

T: I understand. [BLS]. Take a deep breath.

C: Good things in life have a price. I went to Disney and paid a high price to go swimming with the dolphins, but it was really worth it. Most people wouldn't have paid it in order to ride on a dolphin, but I have no regrets. So I am going to pay the price to keep the one with two bedrooms [Laughs].

T: Let's go with that. [BLS]. Take a deep breath. And now?

C: And my mother has nothing to do with this! [Laughs]. She doesn't even know that we will have to pay these five thousand extra and I'm not gong to tell her! [Laughs]. So there!

T: [BLS]

C: Because when I think about it, we really aren't losing. Mathematically speaking, we got a ten thousand bonus. So now, it's reduced to a five thousand bonus, but even so, we still gained five thousand dollars! Which we can use to decorate it. How wonderful! There is still money left over! [Laughs].

T: Wow, having money left over is great! [Laughs]. [BLS].

C: Happiness has a price tag, just like unhappiness. And it is much bigger, and heavier and more expensive than carrying the guilt, which I don't even feel any more. So I am going to hang on to the pleasant feeling, the happiness.

T: So, it's settled?

C: Yes, it's settled.

T: Let's say goodbye to the option that you are discarding?

C: Yes. [BLS].

T: See what you would like to say to it. [BLS].

C: The three-bedroom apartment is going to be full of mold in the winter! [Laughs].

T: That's right! [Laughs]. So you are keeping the two-bedroom option that you can transform into a three bedroom apartment. And what would you like to say to this one?

C: That it is very welcome, and that it makes me happy. It makes me happy that this apartment turned up.

T: And what does it say to you?

C: I'm yours.

T: [BLS]

C: This is mine.

T: And what emotion comes up?

C: Comfort, peace, a desire to be there right now. I can imagine myself decorating it, seeing the sun come up. It's really cool.

T: So, think about that, and feel those feelings. [BLS]. Take a deep breath.

C: And you are invited to come the next time you are in town!

T: So, you can see yourself having company already [Laughs].

C: That's right.

T: Well, thank you very much!

C: This was just great! Thank you!

Dilemma: Marriage or Divorce?

T: Felicity, you said you had a situation that you wanted to resolve?

C: Yes, I'm in a real dilemma. My marriage is on the rocks. When you spoke about people having splinters in their heart, I thought, *my goodness, there are two porcupines living at my house!* [Laughs]. I've thought a lot about whether I should stay in the marriage or leave it. We've been in constant conflicts. I've been especially tense this last month. I'm not sure what to do. I don't know of any way out. So yesterday I thought about doing a session with this dilemma.

T: OK, let's go for it! Let's set up the two options you have. First imagine that you are going to stay in the marriage. What picture comes to mind?

C: Considering the present situation?

T: Yes. You have no guarantee that there will be any changes, especially on his part.

C: That's true. Well, I see myself doing my own thing and he is very distant.

T: And what would be the picture of this?

C: I see myself inside my car, going to work, doing my studies.

T: And if you leave?

C: It's the same picture.

T: I understand. And when you think about this first picture, of staying, what do you think about yourself that is negative, false and irrational?

C: False and irrational? *I have to carry this marriage.*

T: I understand.

C: If I stay in the marriage, I will have to carry it all myself.

T: And if you leave, what would you think about yourself?

C: Well, yesterday I was thinking about all of this. I was thinking what it would be like if I were alone. It's hard to define an irrational belief.

T: So, if you leave, and you are by yourself?

61

C: I think I would feel helpless, but I'm not sure that's it.

T: The Negative Cognition is false and irrational. How about, *I am helpless.*

C: I think that I's better, *I am abandoned.* It makes more sense.

T: OK. And what would you like to think about yourself that is positive?

C: I don't know how to put it into words. What comes to me is an image that I am going to stay, but I am going to be responsible for 50%. I'm not going to continue to carry it all.

T: *I am responsible for my part?*

C: Yes.

T: And if you leave? What's the positive cognition? What do you think about yourself that is positive?

C: I'm going to be free.

T: I'm free?

C: *I'm free.*

T: When you think about this expression, *I am responsible for my part,* and you think about that picture of you in the car, with your stuff, and the option of staying in the marriage, on a scale of one to seven, where seven is completely true and one, completely false, how true do you feel these words, *I am responsible for my part,* are true now?

C: Five.

T: And when you think about the option of leaving, and the words, *I'm free,* on a scale of one to seven, where seven is completely true and one is completely false, how true do you feel these words are when you think about yourself inside the car, free, without your marriage?

C: Also a five.

T: Five. When you think about the first option, the one of staying, what are the emotions that come up for you now? Think about that picture of you in the car; think about the words, *I have to carry it all.*

C: Sadness, loneliness, resentment, anger.

T: OK. And when you think about leaving and you think about this same image, and think about words, *I am abandoned,* what are the emotions that come up for you now?

C: Sadness, and… anguish.

T: When you think about these emotions, sadness, loneliness, resentment and anger, the first option, of staying in the marriage, on a scale of zero to ten, where ten is the greatest distress that you can imagine and zero is none, how much distress do you feel with this option?

C: Eight.

T: And when you think about leaving the marriage, and think about words *I am abandoned,* how much does it bother you now when you think about this?

C: Four.

T: Where do you feel this "eight" in your body? About the first option?

C: In my chest.

T: Where do you feel this "four', this sadness, this anguish about leaving the marriage?

C: In my head.

T: OK. We are going to do some bilateral movements. Let's start with the first option, and then we will do the second one, and then we'll just let it roll, OK?

C: Yes.

T: Let whatever happens, happen. Sometimes we tend to think that things come up that have nothing to do with what we are working on, but let's just let things happen and see how things resolve themselves, OK?

C: Ok. Yes.

T: Let's go! Think about the first option with you in the car.

C: Yes.

T: Think about the words, I have to carry it all.

C: Yes.

T: Feel that in your chest.

C: Yes.

T: And follow the movements. [BLS].

C: I got the feelings here (and places her hand on her chest) that I need to take a deep breath, to see if I can get rid of this feeling.

T: OK. Let's think about the other?

C: OK.

T: So think about leaving the marriage; think about the words, *I am abandoned,* feel it in your head and follow my fingers. [BLS]. Take a deep breath; let it out.

C: I got the feeling that a bunch of things were falling apart in my head, my dreams, my projects, and I got a knot in my throat.

T: Let's keep going?

C: Yes.

T: [BLS]. Take a deep breath; let it out.

C: OK. I started thinking about the two situations, of leaving or staying, and each of your hand movements were a place.

T: I understand.

C: And then I saw myself doing something I realize I have been doing a lot of that, running after him, trying to make him be present, so that he wouldn't be so distant. And then the pain, the sadness the exhustion of all of this, and I thought, *I can't go on the way it is right now.*

T: I understand.

C: It can't go on like this. And then I thought, *it doesn't only depend on me* (cries).

T: Can we keep going? [BLS].

C: I thought of a music that I heard yesterday that says, *I'm not going to cry, you aren't going to cry, you are going to understand that I am not going to see you anymore, at least for now, smile, smile, know that I love you.* I have this feeling. He is just not available. He is very unavailable. I need more space. I need to give it a break. I need more distance, and when I went to talk to him at home about it, he said that if one of us leaves, it's over. There is no going back. But I thought, I need more space, more time. There are things that he is going through. I can't do anything for him, and he is unavailable.

T: I understand.

C: I need more space, more distance.

T: A little while ago you said that you were always running after him. How long do you need to do that?

C: Not any more.

T: Think about that. [BLS].

C: So this question comes up: what am I going to do with what I would like to live? If he isn't available and I am not going to continue to insist anymore, I keep asking myself, what am I going to do? How am I going to stay in this marriage and do what I would like to do, if he is not available to live these things with me?

T: Can you live without his being available to you?

C: With what I would like? [Shakes her head].

T: Go with that. [BLS].

C: My head is hurting, and it seems to have stopped here in the middle, as a Yes. I cannot live these things if he is not available.

T: So, without his being available, it's not possible?

C: For what I want to do with my life, no. For what I would like, no. Without things in common in the relationship? I can't live that way.

T: So go back to the beginning, to the two options. What's it like now?

C: I don't know what to say.

T: Think about that first experience, about staying and see if anything has changed.

C: [Shakes her head.]

T: How much does it bother you now from zero to ten?

C: About a five.

T: And when you think about leaving, has anything changed?

C: No.

T: And how much does it bother you now from zero to ten?

C: Confusion, this feeling that if I let myself be who I am, on one hand, I will be relieved, but on the other, it will bring great pain. So, on one hand the distress level goes down, but on the other, it goes up.

T: It solves one situation, but creates other problems.

C: Yes, that's right.

T: Think about that. [BLS].

C: Several things came up. I feel like I don't want to resolve this now. I'm going to keep on doing what I've done since Friday, since Thursday, really. When the movements [BLS] began, I saw myself inside a kind of cocoon. When I saw myself closing up inside of it, I felt such pain… and I realized that it is an old pain, of staying inside in order to protect myself, so I can survive outside. And I asked myself, *what is this pain?* And I felt the answer was, *No, now it's different. It's not the same as before.* The idea that I need some time is not going to solve the problem. It's clear, it's not defined. It's not simple. I can close myself inside this cocoon, to preserve myself. I got the feeling that I am in my house, closing myself up. It's because I don't want to be in contact with his stuff, with his mess. This is his mess. It's falling on top of us both, like in the marriage, but this is his mess and I don't want it. So that's where the idea came for me to close myself up with my stuff, even at work, with my studies, the things I like, that give me joy, and I'm going to stay inside as long as I need to.

T: Think about this possibility. [BLS].

C: A cocoon with a zipper! [Laughs] or more like a sleeping bag. And I thought, *I'm not responsible for this.* It's not my responsibility to resolve anything that is not my part of the equation. It really is his problem I'm going to stay inside my cocoon to protect myself from his problems, and I'm going to go on with my life. I open the zipper, get my things done, because for now, I think it is a good solution.

T: So maybe we have a third option here? You stay in the marriage but inside your cocoon that has a zipper; you go in and out, without having to be responsible for his stuff.

C: Yes.

T: So, when you think about this cocoon with a zipper, the positive words that you said, *I'm not responsible for his stuff,* are the words you want to use or are there others?

C: I get the feeling of being protected, of comfort, that I can protect myself. I get the idea that I don't have to solve this.

T: Looks like you already did.

C: Yes.

T: Solved it, but in a way that is neither the first or second option; it's a third one. I'm going to stay in the marriage a while longer, but on my terms. In my cocoon that has a zipper. So, when you think about the picture that you have now, and think about positive words, which expression is better? *I am protected. I can protect myself. I can preserve myself?*

C: Really, I think it is *I am safe.*

T: OK. On a scale of one to seven, where seven is completely true and one is completely false, how true do you feel these words, *I am safe*, are when you think about this third option?

C: Five.

T: So I would like for you to think about the cocoon, think about the words, *I am safe*, and follow the movements. [BLS]

C: This is going to be a lot of work.

T: Oh?

C: Yes. Now I feel like, *wow, now I'm going to learn to fly.* [Laughs]. This cocoon has to show up about bedtime, or else I'm going to be beating my wings all day!

T: Yes.

C: What can I do?

T: So, when you think about your cocoon with a zipper, and you think about the words, *I am safe*, how true do you feel these words are now, when you think about this?

C: Seven, I feel safe.

T: [BLS].

C: I feel like going into my cocoon.

T: OK. [BLS]

C: It's a way for me to protect myself, of not losing what I have conquered thus far, my skills, the things I've worked on. It's just a way to protect myself for now. I was afraid of losing myself.

T: And now?

C: No. I hope it works! [Laughs]. I just hope it works.

T: Think about that. [BLS].

C: Wow, I just remembered something from when I was little! When I did this when I was little. It was terrible because I had to go to this place in order to survive. It's a place really deep inside of me. Very painful. It's kinda scary to do this now. It's like: *once again in this place? Am I going to have to do this all of my life?* And then I thought, *no, this time it really is different. It's another time, another place.* I can go inside my cocoon because it's not like a death. It's just an outside layer that I use to protect myself temporarily. At the beginning I went forwards a bit, when I thought, *I hope this works.* Then I saw us doing well, and I thought, *wow, I'm glad I stayed inside, closed up all this time because it preserved many things.*

T: Think about that. [BLS].

C: I think of the picture of me arriving at home, and explaining just the bare minimum to him I'm going to keep to myself. I'm going to use this metaphor of the splinters in the heart. But talking hasn't worked so far. If he gets close to me, his splinters hurt me, like a porcupine. And I am hurting myself as well.

T: So, how is it now?

C: It's good. I just hope that it is possible.

T: On a scale of one to seven, where seven is completely true *I can do this*, what's it like?

C: I can do this? It's a seven. If this is going to resolve it?

T: What do you think?

C: [Laughs] I don't know, because there's his part of the equation. I have my doubts.

T: Yes. Will you be able to do this, yes or no?

C: (Nods).

T: Seven?

C: (Nods).

T: Ok. The consequences are no longer in your hands.

C: No.

T: So, close your eyes just for a moment, think about this *option of the cocoon with a zipper*, you go around doing your own thing, come home at night, and zip yourself up in your cocoon, hoping it will work out. Scan your body, and see if there is any physical discomfort.

C: Here (points to her throat).

68

T: Ok. Pay attention to that. How much does it bother you now?

C: Six

T: OK. [BLS].

C: The image of me vomiting a bunch of stuff that I don't agree with came up. There were so many guilt trips that he would put on me: that I did this, that I did that, that I'm guilty of this, I'm guilty of that. I saw myself throwing up. I am not going to swallow this anymore

T: OK. Now, how is your discomfort?

C: There's something still there. I felt like it went to my stomach. Something left, but something else stayed. I don't know if something moved, but now I have a sensation in my stomach.

T: Positive? Negative?

C: I think it's more negative.

T: How much?

C: A two.

T: Think about that.

C: Can I do it with my eyes closed?

T: Yes. May I do the movement on your hands?

C: Yes.

T: [Therapist stops doing eye movements and does the tactile on her hands.] [BLS].

C: I think the noise inside calmed down. It's the feeling you have after you throw up, but it's not a bad feeling.

T: I understand.

C: Yes. It's nice to be here with myself.

T: And how much does it bother you now from zero to ten?

C: Zero.

T: OK. You know that the reprocessing will often continue after the session.

C: Yes, thank God! [Laughs].

T: And other things may come up.

C: Yes.

T: Sometimes we're not able to see any options as we reprocess. But here we see that a third option appeared. I think that's really interesting. I have a friend who goes to AA [Alcoholics Anonymous] who says that if *nothing changes, nothing changes*. So I think that if you at least try to introduce some kind of change into this system, at least *something* is changing. The way things are right now, we know what to expect. You know that if A, then B; if he does A then C. That's the way things are right now. You have a known and familiar option. So you had to stop and see if you are able to continue living like that, and you said no. It became very clear that you are not able to put up with it like that anymore.

C: Yes, that's true.

T: But the alternative does not have to be a separation. There is another option of staying with him that doesn't hurt you; that doesn't put your marriage in jeopardy. At least it doesn't end the marriage nor destroys it. The option you found gives hope that maybe introducing some change in the system eventually things may come together in a better way.

C: Yes.

T: You always have the option of a separation or divorce. It's there. You also know how to stay with him the way things have been thus far; but it seems that it's worth making an effort of introducing a change that protects you and gives you a greater sense of safety. And who knows, maybe eventually it will change your marriage for the better! That would be really great!

I would like to thank you for sharing this time with us, especially such a difficult issue. Let's see how things will turn out. Keep us posted!

C: I'm the one who thanks you!

Some years later, when I wrote Fernanda to ask her for permission to write this up, and how she eventually resolved her dilemma, this is what she wrote:

Thank you so much for sending me the session so I would watch it. After I read the transcription, I kept seeing this movie going though my head. So many things happened after that session!

Today I am divorced. It was a long process. I lived in a foreign country for six months. I even did a specialization course in trauma!

New loves came and went through my life.

As to the issues regarding my marriage, I'm still cleaning things up inside, especially to free me completely for a new relationships; but now it doesn't bother me anywhere like what I felt when I was married, that sense of not being free to live.

I still long to live a new love, but I can say that I am happier, freer, lighter, in constant movement, as in that important metaphor of being inside my car.

I am finding and accepting new professional challenges with energy and availability. I'm working with EMDR therapy and people who have suffered abuse and violence and I want to specialize more in this field. I have the hope of one day finding someone with whom it would be really worthwhile to share my life.

Thank you. I'm really grateful to you!

What a piece of string can do[2]

T: What would you like to work on today, Rosana?

C: I would like to work on something that happened to me when I was seven years old. I was in the first grade, and I remember the teacher very well. I think that the day before this happened, she said that she was going to take a roll of string to school, and whoever got up out of their chair the next day, she was going to tie them up in their seat. She was teaching class, I did my schoolwork, and then I got up and went to the back of the room. When she arrived in the classroom, she tied me up! She only left this little hand sticking out. It still moves me now that I remember it. [She is visibly moved and tears up.]

T: It is incredible how these things from our childhood still shake us up as adults.

C: And sometime I dream that I'm still encased to this day.

T: So we can have a clear picture to work with, can you describe that snapshot to me?

C: I see myself, all tied up. Tied up, tied up! I'm as tall of the chair, all tied up, all wrapped up in string.

T: And when you think about this difficult experience, Rosana, what words best describe what you think about yourself now that are negative?

C: When I think about that scene? I think about feeling exposed.

T: So, could we say, *I'm vulnerable*?

C: Yes, I am.

T: You also said, *I am encased*?

C: Encased.

T: And I also thought about, *I am tied up*?

C: I am tied up. Yes.

T: Which of these expressions do you think best describes you in this experience?

---

[2] This session is available in Portuguese with English subtitles on YouTube on our channel: https://www.youtube.com/user/emdrbrasil

R: I'm encased.

T: OK. And when you thin you would like to think about yourself now that are positive?

C: I would like to be free.

T: So how can we say that, I'm free? I can be free?

C: I can be free.

T: And when you think about this difficult experience, on a scale of one to seven, where seven is completely true and one is completely false, how much do you feel the positive words, *I can be free*, are true?

C: From zero to seven?

T: On a scale of one to seven.

C: On a scale of one to seven…

T: Seven is completely true and one is completely false.

C: I think it's a seven.

T: When you think about that scene.

C: In that scene? Yes, that's it.

T: So, think about the words, *I can be free*, or, *I'm free*.

C: Ah, *I would like to be free*. [Laughs].

T: Yes, I think that's what you would like, but can we use it in the definitive form? *I am free*? Because that means that you are no longer tied up.

C: Yes. *I'm free*.

T: *I'm free*. So on a scale of one to seven, where seven is completely true and one, completely false, how true do you feel are these words, *I'm free*, now, when you think about that scene?

C: One.

T: And when you think about this difficult experience, and you think about the words, *I'm frozen*, what are the emotions that come up for you now?

C: My heart is really accelerated.

T: What are the emotions?

C: Sadness.

T: Sadness. When you think about this difficult experience, how much does it bother you now, on a scale of zero to ten, where ten is the greatest disturbance that you can imagine and zero is none; when you think about that difficult experience, how much does it bother you now?

C: I think it's a ten, because my heart is ready to come out of my mouth.

T: I was going to ask you where you felt this in your body, but you are telling me that it's in your heart?

C: Yes, I feel it here in my heart.

T: So, go back and think about that difficult experience that you described, think about the negative words, *I'm encased*, see where you feel this in your body and follow my fingers. [BLS]. Take a deep breath; let it out. And now?

C: I think it's a little better.

T: Can we continue?

C: Yes.

T: [BLS]. Take a deep breath; let it out. And now?

C: I feel better. My heart is calming down.

T: OK. Can we continue?

C: [Nods.]

T: Go with that. [BLS]. Take a deep breath. And now?

C: [Laughs] Everything is OK. I'm good.

T: Go back to that difficult experience, and using the scale zero to ten, where ten is the greatest distress that you can imagine and zero is none, how much does it bother you now, when you think about this?

C: It has really gone down. Four. Maybe less. [Laughs].

T: So, how much is it?

C: Two.

T: What is this two?

C: Hmm, this two? What it is? There's something missing… I said I was encased. I think I still need to let go of the rest.

T: Go with that. [BLS]. Take a deep breath; let it out. And now?

C: It's incredible! [Laughs]. It's incredible, but I'm really all right now. It's zero.

T: It's zero. Great! And now when you think about that experience, has something changed? With that little girl?

C: Oh, yes. Yes. It's not important anymore, or not as important. It's in the past. After all, I'm fifty-something, right? This is incredible! It's far away now.

T: Let's do one more round?

C: Yes.

T: [BLS]. Take a deep breath. Let it out.

C: I feel like staying like this, and always looking at your fingers. [Laughs. She s referring to the bilateral visual moment done by the therapist.] The feeling at the and was one of sadness... of looking at that, that scene and feeling relief. Now my heart feels at peace. The tension got better. In the beginning, it seemed like my eyes went faster. They were more anxious. Then I just kept looking at your fingers and I was able to accompany it all better.

T: Now when you go back to that initial experience and think about it on a scale of zero to ten, where ten is the greatest distress and zero is none, how much does it bother you now?

C: Zero. It's far away; it's so far away! [Laughs]. I am not that age anymore. She's far away. I can go by that room. The little girl is very present in that room. And I can just go by her. Once in a while the teacher would tell us stories. She had been my mother's teacher and then later my teacher. She is still alive. Sometimes I think I would like to meet up with her, in an attempt to restore I-don't-know-what. But now I don't need that anymore. I don't need to meet up with her anymore. I don't need to resolve it through her. I feel like it's settled.

T: So, think about that difficult experience with which we began.

C: Ok.

T: Think about the words, *I'm free*; are these the words that you would like to reinforce? Are they still valid or are there other words?

C: Yes, I am free.

T: So, think about this initial experience, think about the words *I'm free,* and on a scale of one to seven, where seven is completely true and one is completely false, how true do you feel these words *I'm free,* are for you now?

C: From? The feeling I have is of being encased, back there looking at the present. I can't say seven, because the chair, the cast, are still there. So I keep imagining that I can't say seven because of that. One to seven? I think there's still something that needs to happen.

T: OK. Go with that.

C: [She tears up and cries during the BLS.}

T: I'm going to continue [the bilateral movements] on your knees, OK?

C: [Nods.]

T: [BLS]. Take a deep breath; let it out.

C: Now that scene really got me. The emotion came up again. It's like this: *I need to, I would like to, I am capable, I'm going to, I need to get out of the chair.* I don't feel like sitting in the chair anymore. [Laughs]. I don't want any more chairs in my life! [Laughs].

T: Can we continue?

C: Yes.

C: My I get up?

T: Of course. Do what you need to.

C: I need to get up.

T: What's happening?

C: I broke off all of the strings! [Laughs]. I broke them all off. Now I can sit down in another state of being. It's like the string went *puft*.

T: How wonderful!!

C: A lot of muscular stuff is happening. I even became fibromyalgic because of this. Not just because of this, but I think it had something to do with it. I was always one to let it out. Now it's like I am receiving the little girl

T: [BLS].

C: So I need to let it out in my body. [Laughs]. I need to stretch. [Stretches in the chair]. Some other images came up, stuff from school, and once again (squeezes both hands together) it comes up again, that feeling of being encased. But it's gotten more diluted now. There. It's gone.

T: OK.

C: Now I've come to the present again. The present is very…. Faithful to what I am feeling. Freedom, that's why I am here [Laughs].

T: YES!

C: That's why I flew, that's why I would like to fly like I have before. It is a victory, a conquest. But I would like to…the feeling now is that it's all turned outwards. Still depending on another to have the authorization to do something.

T: Go with that. ([BLS}.)

C: The image. It's just that it hurt me so much.

T: I understand. Let's check on how it is now?

C: Yes. [Patient hesitates.}

T: You were going to say something?

C: No.

T: Go back to the original experience one more time, and on a scale of zero to ten, where ten is the greatest distress and zero is none, how much does it bother you now when you think about that?

C: Zero.

T: Now when you think about this experience and you think about the words, *I'm free.*

C: I'm free.

T: *I'm free,* on a scale of one to seven, where seven is completely true and one is completely false, how true do you feel these words now, when you think about that? *I'm free.*

C: Being truthful? [Laughs]

T: Being truthful.

C: It's not just being truthful, it's being honest. I think I am almost there.

T: What number is almost there?

C: Six.

T: OK. Let's see you getting there?

C: Of course! [Laughs].

T: Let's go! [BLS].

C: Ah, when you asked me if there was anything else I

wanted to say to her, she came again, but with another feeling. I think that when I went into that scene where I was tied up, I went only in my body. I went through a lot of emotions, and joys as well. And then I got sad. In fact, I still feel sad.

When I got here, the feeling was like this. Once, I went out with my husband. I was really happy. And then I started going home and got sad. I have this a lot: happy/sad. Now I associated it with this thing with being all roped up. My husband tapped me on the shoulder, since he perceived I was sad, with a serious face, and said to me: *Hey! What's going on? I would really like to see the other one.* [Laughs]. I never forgot that scene, so it came up like that. I never forgot that moment, so it came up now. The same feeling from back there, because after this it wasn't just the teacher. There was the story of my dad who would also keep Rosana there. So, looking at this now. All of this came up, my dad, my husband, sadness, tied up in all sorts of ways. I think I need to see it here and look at that story a little longer

T: Can we continue?

C: Yes.

T: [BLS].

C: I need to move physically. I confess that I feel a little bit of fear about the future. Will I be able to get over this one hundred percent? The feeling that this one is... ah, not the one percent. This one is... [nods].

T: Yes? [Laughs]

C: Yes. Of course!! [Laughs]. Of course. *It's over, right!!*

T: OK, so let's confirm it all. Go back to that initial scene, Think about the words, *I'm free,* and on a scale of one to seven, where seven is completely true and one is completely false, how true do you feel these words, *I'm free,* are now with regard to that?

C: I am. Seven.

T: Let's confirm it?

C: Yes, let's do it.

T: [BLS]. Take a deep breath.

C: Incredible, I don't even miss my glasses. [Laughs]. I need to feel this good feeling a little longer.

T: Why for just a little longer?

C: [Laughs] Because I'm afraid this will end, and this feeling will go away.

T: I understand. As if it were something that *I* did instead of something that is yours?

C: I'm afraid of losing your fingers. [Laughs].

T: [BLS].

C: It's mine, isn't it?

T: Yes, it's all yours

C: Yes. I need to hug myself. I think [nods] that I need to do something less muscular. [Rosana get ups from the chair and stretches herself. She walks around the chair once before returning to it and siting down.]

T: OK. Is it a seven?

C: Yes, I'm a seven.

T: Ok, this is what I would like to do. I would like for you to close your eyes for a few moments, think about that difficult experience that we have been working on, think about the positive words, *I'm free,* and examine your body to see if there is still any distress

C: No.

T: Ok. Rosana, as you know the reprocessing that we did today may continue after the session. Take note of anything you want to share here. Give me a ring if you need me. Everything OK?

C: Just great!

T: Is it all yours?

C: It is all mine. It is all mine.

T: Well, congratulations, because it really really is all yours!

C: Thank you!

T: Let me thank you for your generosity and trust in sharing this experience with us.

C: Well, let's enjoy it! [Laughs].

The Blackboard and the Rod: Dealing with the Fear of Math

Problems with math seem to be a very common issue. Unfortunately, many people are limited by what happened to them in school. This case is very typical of these kinds of experiences that we hear in the office.

In this session, it seemed that the resolution of the first situation came very quickly, and Lucy seemed to reprocess quickly and easily. This is something that depends on how each patient reprocesses. There are times where people have repeated experiences with the same issue, so here we had an opportunity to work on other school experiences with the same theme. When we set up a treatment plan for the patient we organize a sequence of goals that we hope to resolve. Although this sequence was not set up at the beginning of the session, Lucy had commented on how she had gone through so many demeaning experiences with math issues. Because of that, once we resolved the first scene fairly quickly, we had time to move into a second scene. This way we went on to a second situation. This way we can show what it's like to "pull the thread" that sometimes connect memories over the same issue.

Therapist: So, Lucy, you already have your safe, calm place [which is a positive resource that can be used during EMDR sessions if the patient needs to rest or slow down before going on with the reprocessing.]

C: Yes.

T: We know which movements you like, and you are aware of the stop sign in case you need to stop. Your metaphor is that of the television. [This is a resource that helps distance the material being reprocessed.] So, I'd like to know what you would like to work on today. You had described a difficult situation to me that happened when you were a child in school. Perhaps you could tell us a little bit more about it...

C: OK. I want to work on an experience I went through when I was in grade school. It went on from first to third grade.

T: About how old were you at the time?

C: I was about seven. I have always been very tall, taller than my peers even at seven. I always sat in the front desk because my father was friendly with the school principal where I studied. He was an intimate friend of the teacher I had from first to third grade. He made it a point of me sitting in the front desk. This was a math teacher that often made me go to the blackboard and do math exercises. When I would make a mistake he would tap a fishing pole on the blackboard, and call me by my last name: *Can-ter-bur-y! You made a mistake! You are dumb!* I would melt with shame in front of my colleagues.

To top it off, I would sit all scrunched up because the friend behind me would keep saying, *You're a giraffe! You're too big! You're too tall! You keep me from seeing the blackboard!* And they would not move me towards the back because my father was friends with the principal and wanted me up front. That marked me profoundly during those three years. I was always on edge during class. I never knew anything about what the teacher was talking about. I just kept waiting for the moment when he would call me up front to the blackboard. Today I am 48 years old and I don't know math. When my kids were going to school, my husband was the one who helped them with their homework/

I have a great desire to learn math. [Laughs] I think it is part of life. When I was doing some course, I would think, *it's a good thing the teacher isn't saying anything about standard deviation!* [Laughs] I don't know anything about stuff that has to do with math. Sometimes when I play around with my kids, I tell them, *don't even ask me, because I can't even add two and two!* So all of this often comes back to mind

T: Ok. When you think about this experience, what image or photograph represents the most difficult part of these experiences? If you were to snap a picture, and describe it to me, what would it be

C: Ah, the photograph of the teacher banging the rod on the blackboard and calling me, Canterbury, you are dumb!

T: When you think about this difficult experience, what are the negative words that best describe what you think about yourself?

C: A word?

T: An expression. I am…

C: Ah, I would be really insecure about myself, I'd be afraid. I was embarrassed in front of all of those students. There were 40 kids in the classroom.

T: But what would the expression be about yourself? *I'm dumb*, like the teacher said? *I'm incapable*?

C: Ah, yes, *I'm dumb in math! I'm dumb in math!*

T: Ok, so let's work specifically with this scene.

C: Yes.

T: So, when you think about this difficult experience, what words best describe what you would like to think about yourself that are positive?

C: Ah, I would like to think about having the teacher call me up front to the blackboard and I could do the exercise. Then everyone would say, *wow! Look how smart she is!*

T: I'm smart?

C: Yes!

T: Now, when you think about this experience, on a scale of one to seven, where seven is completely true and one is completely false, how true do you feel these positive words are, *I am smart*, when you think about this now?

C: Ah, one. One or zero.

T: There's no zero On a scale of one to seven.

C: One.

T: So you don't believe you are smart at all with regard to this?

C: With math? No way.

T: And when you think about this experience and these negative words, *I'm dumb*, what are the emotions that you feel now?

C: Insecurity.

T: And when you think about this difficult experience, how much does it bother you now on a scale of zero to ten, where ten is the highest distress you can imagine and zero is nothing?

C: Seven.

T: Where do you feel this distress in your body?

C: Here in my heart.

T: Ok, then let's get started, you know about the stop sign, and that each person has their own way of processing. Just let whatever happens, happen and just watch. Ready?

C: Ready.

T: So, think about the image of this difficult memory, think about the negative words *I'm dumb*, feel this in your body, and follow the movements. [BLS].

T: Take a deep breath; let it out. And now, what comes up?

C: Everything is the same.

T: Let's keep going? [BLS] Take a deep breath. [Client laughs] What happened?

C: I saw myself doing the exercises! [Laughs].

T: Really?

C: My teacher didn't bang the rod on the blackboard anymore.

T: Really? Very well. Let's go with that.

C: OK.

T: [BLS]. Take a deep breath, let it out. And now?

C: It was very good. Everybody got up, and applauded me. I was able to do the exercise and the teacher gave me a hug.

T: Ah, that is beautiful! Just beautiful! So, Lucy, go back to that difficult experience. On a scale of zero to ten, where zero is no distress that you can imagine, how much does it bother you now?

C: I can't even see the teacher banging the rod on the blackboard anymore.

T: OK.

C: All I can see now is the teacher smiling and coming to hug me.

T: Wow, that's just great!

C: I think it's a zero. A zero… or a one.

T: Zero or one? This scale goes from zero to ten. Is it a zero or a one?

C: Zero.

T: Zero is no distress

C: Yes, that's right.

T: Is that how you feel?

C: Yes.

T: OK. Now, go back and think this difficult memory that we started with, are the words, *I'm smart*, are still valid? Do they relate to what you are experiencing or are there other words you would like to use?

C: That's positive?

T: Yes.

C: No, I think it's, *I'm smart.*

T: Very well. Think about this experience and the words *I'm smart*, on a scale of one to seven, where seven is completely true and one is completely false. How much do you feel these positive words are true now?

C: Seven.

T: Really?

C: Yes.

T: So, think about this difficult experience, think about the words, *I'm smart* and follow the movements.

C: OK.

T: [BLS]. Take a deep breath.

C: [Client claps her hands and laughs]. *I'm smart!* I was able to do it all!

T: Really?!

C: It was very beautiful.

T: That is just great! So you were able to go to the blackboard and do all of the math problems?

C: I went and I did them all. And I wasn't all scrunched up. I was standing tall.

T: So your height isn't an issue?

C: No.

T: So, one more time, on a scale of one to seven, where seven is completely true and one is completely false, how true do you feel these words are, *I'm smart*?

C: Seven.

T: So, close your eyes for a moment. Think about that difficult experience that we have just worked on... do a body scan. See if there is any distress in your body or if it has all cleared up.

C: My heart doesn't beat fast anymore.

T: Any distress?

C: No.

T: Lucy, we could end the session here, but we still have some time in our session. I thought maybe we could work on some of the other memories that are related to this and that still bother you. Do you remember another similar instance where something like this happened? With regard to math

C: Yes, I remember.

T: Tell me about it?

C: It was in the eighth grade. I got a 2 out of 10 on the math test. It was the worse grade I ever got in my whole life. When I got home, my dad really spanked me, because he said he had paid a lot of money for a private tutor and that I should have gotten at least an eight on the test.

T: How old were you at the time?

C: I was thirteen going on fourteen.

T: I understand. And when you think about this experience what are the negative words that you think about yourself now?

C: Ah, my father was always saying: *Yeah, you are never going to amount to anything. You're not going to get ahead in life. You are dumb. You don't study. Look at your brother, and how smart he is. He always gets ten in math. I'm wasting all this money on you with private tutors and you still can't learn.*

T: So, what would be the negative belief here? *I'm dumb? I'm incapable?*

C: That I will never amount to anything; that I am incapable.

T: Which is better? *I'm never going to amount to anything* or *I'm incapable?*

C: *I'm never going to amount to anything.*

T: and when you think about this difficult experience that you are describing, what words best describe what would you like to think about yourself that are positive?

C: A word?

T: An expression; a positive belief about what would you like to think about yourself. Instead of thinking, *I'm never going to amount to anything,* what would you like to think about yourself that is positive?

C: Ah, that even in secret, I could help make people happy.

T: How could we say that in a short positive way? *I am capable? I can help others? I can do it? I am somebody? I'm important?*

C: *I am somebody to someone.*

T: OK. And when you think about this situation with your dad, and you think about the positive words, *I am somebody to someone,* on a scale of one to seven, where seven is completely true and one is completely false, how true do you feel these words are, *I am somebody to someone,* regarding this now?

C: Three.

T: And when you think about this experience with your dad, and think about negative words, *I'm never going to amount to anything,* what feelings come up for you now?

C: A great dissatisfaction; a desire to please my dad; a desire to correspond to his expectations about me.

T: What emotions do you feel when you hear him say these things to you?

C: Anger.

T: And when you think about this difficult experience, how much does it bother you now on a scale of zero to ten, where ten is the greatest distress that you can imagine and zero is none.

C: Five.

T: Where do you feel this in your body?

C: Here also (points to her heart).

T: So, I would like for you to go back and think about this difficult experience, think about the words *I'll never amount to anything,* feel this in your body and follow my fingers.

87

T: [BLS]. Take a deep breath. What comes up for you now?

C: Nothing; just my heart beating.

T: What does your heart-beating mean?

C: Fear.

T: Go with that. [BLS]. Take a deep breath. And now?

C: Anxiety.

T: Let's keep going? [BLS]. Take a deep breath; let it out. And now?

C: [Client talks as if she were talking to her dad in the scene she is working on.] *Look, Dad, I really did get a two, but I am going to learn. Some day I will learn it.*

T: Let's keep going? [BLS]. Take a deep breath.

C: Hey, Dad I got an eight! [Laughs] I saw the number eight in the corner of the test.

T: Really?

C: In red..

T: Wow, that's great! Let's continue a little bit more? [BLS]. Take a deep breath. Let it out. And now?

C: I saw Mrs. Smith giving me my test. She was my math teacher in the eighth grade. I got a 9,5 and she was congratulating me. Mrs. Smith, the teacher, she was a man, with boots and everything because she was a rancher. She only rode a pickup, wore a ponytail, and a hat. She gave me my test and it was a 9,5!

T: Wow!!!

C: I wonder why it is that the images that most made an impression on me were men or images of men. Mrs. Smith was homosexual. Back then nobody talked about these things, but people whispered about it in the corridors. She gave me my test, and then called me to the principal's office because my father went there to see the test. She put my test in my father's hands.

T: Let's go back to the difficult experience. Now on a scale from zero to ten, where ten is the greatest distress that you can imagine, and zero is none, how much does it bother you now when you think about that?

C: No, it doesn't bother me.

T: When you think about this second experience that we are working on, about your dad and think about words *I am somebody to someone,* are these words still valid or would you like to use another expression?

C: *I have importance to someone.*

T: I have importance. So think about the initial experience, and the words, *I have importance to someone,* and on a scale of one to seven, where seven is completely true and one is completely false, how much do you feel these positive words are true now?

C: Seven.

T: So think about this difficult experience, think about the words, *I have importance to someone,* and follow my fingers.

C: Say again?

T: Think about that difficult experience, with your dad.

C: When I got a 2?

T: Yes. And think about the words, *I have importance to someone.* Put those two things together.

C: Right.

T: And follow my fingers. [BLS]. Take a deep breath.

C: The 2 isn't important anymore, because there are people calling me [Laughs] so I can go to work for them.

T: So, when you think about this difficult experience with your dad, on a scale of zero to ten, where ten is the greatest distress and zero is none, is it still a zero?

C: Yes.

T: And when you think about the words, *I have importance to someone*, on a scale of one to seven.

C: Seven.

T: Seven is completely true and one is completely false?

C: Still a seven.

T: Very well. Now think about this difficult experience, think about the words, *I have importance to someone,* and scan your whole body and see if there is any distress anywhere.

C: No.

T: So, Lucy, one more time, just to remind you that the reprocessing may continue after the session. I'd like to ask you something, just out of curiosity. Now, when you think about learning math, how much do you think it is possible?

C: I know I can do it.

T: And if I talk about standard deviation you wouldn't tremble anymore?

C: [Laughs] No.

T: You're going to learn statistics?

C: Right.

T: And when you think about going to class?

C: I can see myself doing the numbers, with those long columns of numbers that fill up two pages in order to resolve them.

T: Great. Thank you so much for your time and willingness to work with us on this. It was really nice to work together.

C: Thank you.

Some years later, I wrote Lucy and asked her about her math issues. When she left that session she had said she was going to have to go to a specialized math class in order to learn the math basics, since she couldn't even add. But look what she wrote back:

Esly, I'm going to be really sincere with you. When I would think about that teacher [with the rod] I hated him; but after the session, the hatred was gone. And I can teach math to my adolescents in the consulting office. I can even help my grandson with his math homework! It was really worth it!

Untangling

T: So, what would you like to work on today?

C: It's an anxiety that I feel when someone approaches me about an issue for which I am ill prepared or that I wasn't expecting. Even when I know something about the subject, I get all tangled up in my head.

T: I understand.

C: It seems like all of the words get tangled up together and I can't find the right answers.

T: Do you remember when you first felt this?

C: I've been able to make a few associations. I had a lot of trouble learning arithmetic. To this day I don't understand it well. I have to count on my fingers or use other strategies. Learning the math tables was a drama in my life. I think elementary school is always complicated, having to learn the math tables. I remember being in second grade and the teacher would test us about it. But she would surprise us. It was really bad, because I never knew if she was going to call on me or not. I knew I had not been able to learn that content. So for me it was always trying to memorize without understanding what was happening to me. When I was a child, it seemed like the numbers would mix together. So there was this bunch of numbers dancing in my head and I couldn't answer. Second and third grade were really hard for me because of math. I didn't have problems with the other classes, but arithmetic was a real issue...!

I remember once when we were going through that phase where she would call me to the blackboard to solve a math problem. It was something simple. If I could have kept my cool, I think I probably could have solved it, but the fact that she called me up front made all of the numbers jumble together. I didn't know if I was supposed to add, or subtract or multiply. I couldn't see a thing. One time I went up front and just stood there, without knowing what to do. I just wrote down any number because I just couldn't think. Now that I remember this... maybe that's the issue. People catch me off guard and I can't think. It's like I lose my head and it all goes into my stomach. I just couldn't do the exercise. I didn't get it right and the teacher caught me by my pony-tail and threw me down onto the floor. I was really embarrassed in front of my friends and colleagues. It was really bad because it had happened other times where she would surprise us with math problems. I just couldn't learn the addition and subtraction and stuff.

T: So we have a clear incident. Do you remember how old you were at the time the teacher picked you up by the hair?

C: I think I was about eight. It was second grade.

T: And when you think about this image, what negative words express what you think about yourself now?

C: Ah, I feel shame and confusion. I got really confused.

T: And what would you say about a person that is ashamed?

C: Ah, I think all of this is really complicated.

T: A complicated person?

C: They are complicated situations.

T: But what do you think about yourself? There you were, at the blackboard, ashamed, with all of this stuff that you are feeling.

C: And this fear.

T: Fear.

C: Fear of not being able to do it.

T: But what do you think about yourself. You are describing what you feel. What do you think about yourself that is negative? *I'm dumb? I'm incapable? I can't do it?*

C: I think incapable. *I'm incapable.*

T: And if I had a magic wand here and I were able to resolve all of this, what would you like to think about yourself that is positive regarding this issue?

C: Something positive about all of this?

T: Yes, about yourself.

C: I would like to have the clarity of mind today, *this content I know, and this one I don't understand.* Nowadays, when these unexpected moments come up – because all of this happens usually when I am caught by surprise – I know I know, but I can't organize my ideas. I know it, but the words run together and my ideas get tangled up.

T: So how could we say this? *I can think with clarity? I'm capable? I can do it?*

C: I think my greatest desire is, *I can think with clarity.*

T: Very well. And when you think about that picture that you described, how true do you feel are these positive words *I can think with clarity,* on a scale of one to seven, where one you feel to be completely false and seven is completely true?

C: For that time?

T: For that incident.

C: For that day? It's a zero.

T: The lowest number on this scale is a one.

C: Well, it's negative, extremely negative.

T: Completely false. *I'm not capable. I can't think with clarity.* You had said that when you think about this image, you feel shame and confusion. And you mentioned fear. What emotions do you feel when you think about that incident? Shame? Fear? Confusion?

C: Yes.

T: And on a scale of zero to ten, where ten is the greatest distress that you can imagine and zero is no distress, how much does it bother you now, when you think about that?

C: Think about that picture?

T: Yes.

C: Nowadays it doesn't bother me so much, that picture of the teacher suspending me in the air by my hair. It doesn't bother me so much. I'd say a four, but the confusion is something I still feel very strongly even now.

T: So how much would the confusion be?

C: Ah, the confusion is an eight or nine.

T: Where in your body do you these things?

C: The confusion? In my head.

T: And this event that we are working on?

C: In my chest.

T: So I would like for you to think about this difficult experience that you have just described to me about the teacher, see yourself at the blackboard, think about the negative words, *I am incapable,* see where you feel this in your body and follow the

93

movements. [BLS]. What happened? [Therapist perceives that something had happened to the client]

C: There's a pain in my chest.

T: Can we continue?

C: [Nods.]

T: Think about that. Remember that you can always ask me to stop. [BLS].

C: What comes up for me is, *why does this only happen to me?* I feel very different from everybody else. I thought it only happened to me.

T: Can we keep going? [Clients nods] [BLS]. Take a deep breath; let it out. And now?

C: I think my body feels lighter now.

T: Let's keep going?

C: Yes.

T: [BLS]. Take a deep breath. What's it like now?

C: I'm feeling more integrated with my physical body now.

T: So, when you think about this difficult experience with which we started, on a scale of zero to ten, where ten is the greatest distress you can imagine, and zero is none, how much does it bother you now?

C: I think a five.

T: What is this five?

C: This five…. I think there's still something there. I need to know that it's easier for me.

T: Think about that. [BLS]. Take a deep breath. And now?

C: I think it went down to a three.

T: What is this three?

C: There is still this fear of not being able to organize my thoughts. I'm worried that I won't be able to do it.

T: Go with that.

C: Yes. [BLS].

T: And now?

C: It's a two.

T: What is this two?

C: I'm concerned that things may get tangled up again later on. But I can already think more clearly.

T: Let's keep going? [BLS].

T: Take a deep breath. And now?

C: I think it's a one.

T: What is this one?

C: It's a concern of not being able to remember some things, but it seems that the organization is getting better.

T: [BLS]. Take a deep breath. And now?

C: I think it's a zero.

T: You think?

C: Yes, I think so.

T: That's great! Now, go back to that first picture. Has anything changed?

C: Yes, it has.

T: What's different?

C: It's like the curtain closed over that. I know that it's still there, but it's just shadows behind the curtain. It's not something clear, visible or identifiable.

T: [BLS]. Take a deep breath. And now?

C: It cleared up

T: And when you think about this experience now on a scale of zero to ten, where ten is the greatest distress and zero is none?

C: That event doesn't bother me anymore.

T: Now when you think about this difficult experience, that we have been working on, and you think about the words, *I can think with clarity* on a scale of one to seven, where seven is completely true and one, completely false, how true do you feel these words are now?

C: This minute?

T: Yes, this minute.

C: I think it's a seven.

T: Now then, I would like you to think about that incident with the teacher. Think about the positive words, *I can think with clarity*, and follow my fingers. [BLS].

T: Take a deep breath. And now?

C: [Nods.]

T: What does that mean?

C: *I can think with clarity*

T: Great! A powerful seven?

C: Yes.

T: So, one more time. Go back to that experience, think about the words, *I can think with clarity*. Everything OK?

C: Yes.

T: Powerful seven?

C: Powerful seven!

T: OK. Close your eyes for a moment, think about that incident. Think about the positive words, I *can think with clarity*, and mentally scan your body, from head to foot, and tell me if there is any distress.

C: No.

T: Great. The processing that we did today may continue after the session. It may happen that during the week, you may have new insights, thoughts, memories and dreams. If this happens, just pay attention to what is coming up for you, what you see, feel, think and identify the triggers. Take note of these things that come up during the week and bring it to the next session. We can work on them in our next session, if necessary. Remember that you can use your safe/calm place that we installed, to help you with any discomfort that might appear. If necessary, please feel free to give me a ring, OK?

C: OK.

T: Now then, out of curiosity, when you think about some of those things that would make your thoughts get tangled up, what's it like now?

C: The tangling thing doesn't bother me anymore. It's funny how now it doesn't bother me anymore. Before, I would get nervous. But I think I'll only really be certain when I face another situation like that and know that this is really gone. I still feel a bit of insecurity.

T: What's that insecurity like? Let's work on it for just a few more moments?

C: Yes, of course.

T: OK. [BLS]. Take a deep breath. And now? What happened [The client had a reaction.]

C: [Laughs] I'm calmer. It's just a little dot.

T: A little dot?

C: Yes, just a little dot.

T: From zero to ten, how much does it bother you now?

C: The insecurity?

T: Yes.

C: I think it's a zero.

T: And when you think about the future, and think about a situation that could come up where you would normally feel your thoughts getting tangled up, what's that like?

C: What I would like for the future is to be able to think clearly.

T: And when you see yourself in the future, so you see yourself with clarity or not?

C: Yes, I see myself.

T: And how do you see yourself?

C: The clarity of knowing that there are things that I remember and things I don't. The clarity of knowing that there are things I don't remember.. it's not because it got all tangled up, or that the words mixed together. It's just that the old memory has faded [Laughs].

T: Great!

C: Faded. And it's not that things are tangled up. The things I remember come clearly, like a clear text. I remember and I understand. That's the future.

T: That's the future. That's the future that awaits you! [Laughs]. Well, I really want to thank you. It's been a privilege to work with you.

Comments:

One of the interesting things that happened in this session was that we had the time and opportunity to help the client see herself in the future. The three-pronged protocol of EMDR therapy helps us identify what needs to be worked on in the past, the triggers in the present that often contribute to maintaining unwanted behavior, and a future (ideal) template. The client had the opportunity of "seeing herself" reach her desired results. What we like to see in this form of processing is the client able to perceive themselves developing healthy and functional behavior that was out of their reach before.

My First Kiss

The initiation of a person's romantic life does not always start off on the right foot. Clare shares with us some of the difficulties she faced. It is worth noting in this session that sometimes the parents' response can be even more complicated than the difficult experience itself.

One of the beautiful things about EMDR therapy is how it also protects the client. There are situations where people are ashamed about what happened to them or too embarrassed to give the details of what occurred. With this kind of therapy it is not necessary what the client thinks about the experiences during the bilateral movements. That is how the brain can find the neural file in order to reprocess it.

We will also see how something that happened during Clare's adolescence and had been limiting her relationships as an adult was resolved in less than an hour. It was a moving, delicate and sacred moment.

T: So let's go, Clare. What would you like to work on today?

C: Let me go direct to the scene. I ended my last romantic relationship about five years ago, and nothing more has ever happened. Everything is complicated. So the scene I would like to work on is the one of my first kiss. I was about eleven or twelve years old. It was like this:

I was still a kid, a tomboy. I would play in the streets. I was still a child. I was just beginning to wake up to the fact that there were boys in the world. Everything was all right in the beginning. I liked to play, but in my circle of friends, most of the girls had already been with the boys, kissed them and stuff. I was just fine with the way I was. I had just begun to get attracted to a boy who lived in town. I had a friend who had a real issue with the fact that I still hadn't kissed anybody. I shared with her in confidence about my new feelings and she used that information to tell the guy about it.

One day she told me to be in such and such a place at a certain time to meet up with her, so we could get together to play a sport I really liked at the time. But instead of finding her when I got there, the boy was there. I didn't have the resources to do anything. He just came up to me, put his arms around me and started kissing me. I froze. I wasn't expecting that. I totally froze, and I stayed frozen the whole time. I wasn't able to to respond even to set boundaries with the guy. This scene in itself was horrible. I stood there until he said, *Ok, now go home. I'll see you later.* For him, everything was fine. He didn't even perceive how horrified I was. All I wanted to do was go back home. I remember it was raining and I had an umbrella the whole time.

If there were a way to kill myself, I think I would have done it right then, because I was feeling so awful. I kept it together enough to keep from screaming and yelling down the street to my house. Finally, I got home. I think I spent two hours taking a bath, washing myself off. All that was going through my head was, *This is the end. This is the end.* That's how the day ended. Something inside of me died, you know? I cried uncontrollably.

I figured out about the time my parents would come home from work. I didn't want them to see me like that. I locked myself in my bedroom. I just cried and cried. My parents wound up hearing me. They got really worried. I was so ashamed. I didn't want to open the door. My face was all swollen from crying. Finally my mom insisted so much I had to open the door. She saw me like that. I couldn't control myself. When I saw her I got even more upset. It was a long time before I was even able to tell her what had happened. But... because of how hysterical I was, she didn't realize that all that had happened was just a kiss. She was very very worried. She totally lost her good sense. She took me to her bedroom..

I can still see this scene with all of its details. She asked my dad to leave the room. I was already in my pajamas. She took off my pajama pants, my underwear and spread my legs apart to see if I had been raped. Of course I hadn't! But if there were some part of me that hadn't frozen yet, it totally froze then.

T: Oh, my goodness. What difficult experiences! With which of the two experiences do you want to start?

C: I've worked on this story several times in several ways. I think the part with the boy is worse. The worse parts have to do with my girlfriend, because I only found out later that she had set this up. Up until then I blamed myself. The part about my mom was bad, too...

T: So, do you want to start with the experience with the young boy or with your mom? You said that you froze when the boy approached you, and that what still hadn't been frozen, froze up with your mom.

C: Yes. The part with my mom is worse.

T: OK. So it would be when you think this image of your mom examining you?

C: Yes.

T: When you think about this, what do you think about yourself that is negative, false and irrational?

C: I don't know how to put this in words very, but it's like, *I ruined everything, I did something very wrong.*

T: I ruined my life. My life is ruined?

C: It's ruined.

T: It is ruined forever?

C: I'm not worth anything.

T: I'm not worth anything.

C: From that moment on, I'm not worth anything.

T: Ok. So it would be, *I'm not worth anything?*

C: [Nods]. Can I leave it like, *My life is ruined,* because that's what I think I am.

T: You choose.

C: Then that's it.

T: OK. *My life is ruined.* If I had a magic wand that would help you transform it into something positive, what would you like to think about yourself that is positive?

C: Something like, *I can still have a good relationship.*

T: Ok. *I can still have a good relationship.* And when you think about this difficult experience, on a scale of one to seven, seven is completely true and one is completely false, how true do you feel these positive words, *I can still have a good relationship*, are now?

C: Two.

T: And when you think about this difficult experience and think about negative words, *My life is ruined*, what are the emotions that come up for you now?

C: Sadness, anger, because I think about that friend. Disgust, disgust, disgust. Disgust with myself, disgust with that guy. Anger at my mom, for her not being able to deal with her daughter in a better way.

T: Ok. And when you think about this difficult experience, how much does it bother you now, on a scale of zero to ten, where ten is the greatest distress that you can imagine and zero is no distress?

C: It has been a ten, but now that I think about it, I think it's a nine.

T: Where do you feel that in your body?

C: I feel a suffocation in my lungs, in my chest, really tight. It comes and goes, with a feeling of disgust in my stomach. I've had situations where I thought I would throw up.

T: OK, Clare. You know how this works, so are you ready to start?

C: (Nods affirmatively).

T: Any questions?

C: No.

T: So, go back and think about that picture, of this experience with your mom. Think about the negative words *My life is ruined*, see where do you feel this in your body and follow the movements. [BLS]. Take a deep breath, let it out. And now?

C: It came back.[Client cries.]

T: Can we continue? Remember you can always ask me to stop if you need to, OK?

C: Yes.

T: Remember it's old stuff. Just look at it, and let it go. Yes. [BLS]. Take a deep breath. Let it out.

C: What came to me was the scene of my birth, and really good aspects of my mom's maternity, but it's strange.

T: Can we continue?

C: [Nods.]

T: [BLS]. Take a deep breath.

C: I keep looking at this scene and this time I didn't cry nor did it give me that despair I felt before.

T: Now when you think about this experience, on a scale of zero to ten, where ten is the greatest distress and zero is none, how much does it bother you now?

C: Six.

T: What is this six?

C: Accept that this is what happened.

T: OK. Think about that. [BLS].

C: At first, a sadness came up, but then a filling up started. Warmth.

T: Let's keep going? Go with that. [BLS].

C: Really good feelings about myself started to appear, but immediately I felt a great fear of showing it.

T: Go with that. [BLS].

C: It just increases. There are moments that this phrase comes to me: *you don't need to keep in so many good things that you have inside yourself. You don't need to be so mean to yourself.* I don't need to be afraid anymore.

T: Yes! [BLS].

C: Ah, once again I got the scene of when I was born, of my arrival, and there was so much love! I can almost see this love spilling over.

T: That's beautiful!

C: I'm moved.

T: Good! That is so wonderful! Clare, go back and think about that initial scene that we are working on. On a scale of zero to ten, where ten is the greatest distress and zero is none, what is it now?

C: Zero.

T: Has anything changed?

103

C: It's like my posture with regard to this now is one of just looking at it. I remember all of it. That's the way it was.

T: Yes, that's the way it was.

C: But, it doesn't keep me from anything, from being who I am and all of the possibilities that exist for my life.

T: That's true. So, now when you think about this difficult experience and you think about the words, *I can have a good relationship*, are these the words that you would like to reinforce or are there others?

C: Well, it turned into something more general, not just with regard to a romantic relationship, but something similar. And yet, at the same time, more significant: *I can show my love.*

T: Lovely! Now, when you think about that in that experience with your mom, and think about the words, *I can show my love*, on a scale of one to seven, where seven is completely true and one is completely false, how true do you feel these positive words are now?

C: Five.

T: So, bring up that difficult experience, think about the words, *I can show my love*, and follow the movements. [BLS]. Take a deep breath.

C: Yes. What I still think isn't good doesn't have to do with my mom, but love for myself. It was always the non-expression of this love for myself that kept me from setting healthy boundaries: in abusive friendships; with the boy with whom I wasn't ready for that, or with my mom. I could have said, we don't need all of this. It's not a matter of lack of strength, but not being able to express love for myself. Once again the scene of my birth comes up.

T: Now when you think about that difficult experience, and think about words, *I can show my love*, on a scale of one to seven, where seven is completely true and one is completely false, how true do you feel these words are now with regard to that?

C: There is a part that is still a six.

T: OK.

C: Like some insecurity...

T: Go with that. [BLS]. Take a deep breath.

C: There finally came a mixture of images of tons of things in my childhood: me as a child, real mischievous. And a phrase came up: *I deserve this love.*

T: Go with that. [BLS].

C: [Tears up.] She didn't take care of herself. The little girl didn't take care of herself. I often have this feeling, when I really empathize with another person. Now I'm having that experience with myself.

T: How wonderful! So –

C: Seven [Laughs].

T: Seven?

C: Seven! Seven!

T: Let's go one more round and turn it into a powerful seven?

C: Yes, let's do that! I need to.

T: Let's go. [BLS].

C: Now I got the feeling that I have the necessary containment for all of this love. I thought maybe I had too much love; that I would get lost in the middle of it all.

T: [BLS]. [Client takes a deep breath].

C: I'm at peace!

T: Great. Close your eyes just for a moment. Think about this difficult experience that we have just worked on and think about the positive words, *I can show my love.* Slowly examine all of your body and tell me if you feel any disturbance.

C: No. I'm at peace. It's like there's room for everything now here inside. Everything is organized. It's a really good feeling. There is room for other people, too, now.

T: Just great! Clare, the reprocessing that we did today may continue after the session, as you well know. If you need anything, just get in touch with me.

C: Yes. Thank you!

T: What a wonderful gift you are taking with you.

C: Super. Thank you.

T: You are beautiful. Thank you for trusting me with such a difficult and delicate issue. All the best to you!

C: Thank you. [Laughs].

We ended the session, but since this was a live demonstration in a class setting, we started talking about the methodological reprocessing and the comments. A half hour later, seeing how her face had cleared up, I asked Clare:

T: How are you feeling now?

C: It's difficult. Now I think I will have to work on the other scene, with the boy.

T: Now when you think about that scene, has anything changed?

C: Yes, it has. I feel like using my new resources on him! [Laughs].

T: Close your eyes for a moment. Finish that scene the way you would have liked for it to finish.

C: This was a boy that I was beginning to get interested in, but I wasn't ready.

T: Let the little girl talk. [A few minutes of silence while the client thinks about the scene when the boy kissed her.]

C: Yes, everything is all right. Maybe next time I'll have a good time with him! [Laughs].

T: Way to go! [Laughs].

C: Yes, but it will happen when *I want it*, when I am ready.

T: Exactly, when you are ready.

C: Now I'm going to my friend's house..

T: Yes, let's give her a piece of your mind! [Laughs].

C: [Laughs] I told her it was ok for us to be different, but everybody had their own timing. I told her [in my imagination] that I accepted the fact that she had had her experiences, and that I could learn from them, but for me, it wasn't time yet. I still liked to play.

T: *I still like playing with dolls!* [Laughs].

C: That's right! Now I'm going to my house, smiling. This is just great!

T: You can see that the reprocessing can be spontaneous. I wanted to propose this experience to you before, but we were running out of time. See how one scene draws another one. And you were able to give the story with the fellow an ending that you wanted. That brings closure.

C: That's true.

We always alert our clients that the reprocessing may continue after the session. It was very interesting to see Clare's physical expressions change. I perceived the changes in her posture and expressions which was why I asked her to try and finalize the other scene as well.

It is also important to remember that one of the things that complicates trauma is precisely the "unfinished step." Because of my previous training in Psychodrama, I often propose to my EMDR clients to do what I call an "Internal Psychodrama" while reprocessing with bilateral movements. I use cognitive interweaves based on what emerges spontaneously from the client, especially questions that are solution-based[3], as a way of bringing closure to the unfinished step. In this case I used the technique by asking the client to finish the scene, but with a desired ending. It is a way of giving the client what was needed to finish. Since the brain doesn't always differentiate, between what really happened and what was imagined, it is a way of bringing resolution to a difficult experience.

---

[3] Esly Carvalho, Ph.D. – *Solution-Based Cognitive Interweaves*©

Fear of Chickens

T: So, Mary Francis, tell me a little bit about what you want to work on today.

C: It's something I find interesting. Last night, after talking to you, I dreamt a whole bunch of interesting stuff. I had a family that did not offer me to go places I really wanted to go. There was a time when my dad just disappeared. All of this came to me last night.

Remember that I told you that I wanted to work on my fear of chickens? It's because I'm ashamed of admitting I have this fear. Even my nephews laugh at me and say, *Auntie, why are you afraid of chickens?* It was about this time [when my father disappeared], I went to pick up a chicken and it got stuck here on my chest. I was so paralyzed with fear that I couldn't get the chicken off. I just froze. Last night I had nightmares about this time of my life. My father disappeared, my mother has been depressed for as long as I can remember, and so I lacked a safe place. I went to live with my maternal grandmother which was horrible. I remember my grandfather coming home with a bag, and in this bag there was powdered milk; there was food. So whenever things get difficult, I seek refuge in food. This has been a real problem because now I have high cholesterol. I can't control myself. So when I get anxious, I seek my safe place in food, seeking love in food.

T: You had mentioned working on your fear of chickens. Is that what you would like to work on?

C: The chicken is tied to this because it all happened about the same time.

T: OK.

C: My father disappeared, and my mother was sick and I had to go get this chicken, and it hung on my shirt, but I think the reason I paralyzed in that situation was because I didn't have anybody! What was going on?

T: The two things mixed together…

C: Yes, all of this got mixed up with the chicken. I don't know how to explain it.

T: Well, you know about the stop sign, and that we can stop whenever you like. You chose the train as your metaphor. We've tested the bilateral movements, and you have your safe place. You mentioned that you froze as a result of having the chicken hanging on your front, without being able to do anything... is that the worst picture? The most difficult part of this experience? Or is there a moment when the fear of chickens is worse?

C: The worst part is feeling paralyzed in the face of what happens to me, and seeking refuge in food. I always do that.

T: I'm looking for a picture. Can we use the picture of the chicken?

C: Maybe my grandfather, carrying the bag of food. It's stronger than the chicken scene.

T: If we work on the experience of your grandfather with the bag we may not heal the fear of chickens.

C: I'd rather deal with the food issue. I can go without dealing with the chicken. [Laughs]. Let's leave the chicken for later.

T: So, give me a further description of what this picture is like, as if it were a photograph.

[See the importance of getting it really clear about what we are going to work on. The client is always right! They can even change their minds during session.]

C: It's a street where I used to live, a dead-end street.

T: I understand.

C: A narrow alley, and I see my grandfather coming from far away with a blue bag in his hand. I know there is food inside, and I run to meet him. That is the strongest visual image.

T: When you think about this image, this difficult experience, what do you think about yourself now that is negative?

C: It's this thing I've worked on for years, in therapy and stuff, that I can't control this thing with food. I feel helpless in the face of my anxiety that makes me eat everything.

T: So, could we say, *I'm helpless*? Are those the words that best describe yourself?

C: It's like a chaos comes up. The anxiety draws me in a lot. It was a time of chaos like: there's not going to be enough to eat. There's going to be a lack of people, a lack of everything...

T: And... I'm helpless?

C: And I'm helpless.

T: When you think about this image, this difficult experience, what would you like to think about yourself now that is positive, instead of, *I'm helpless*?

C: That I have control over my acts, over my anxiety. I think it's more my anxiety than my behavior. It's dealing with the anxiety that I feel more helpless.

T: Let's see if we can put this in more general terms. How about: *I have self-control? I am in control?*

C: *I am in control.* Control is the key word.

T: When you think about this image that you described about your grandfather with the blue bag, how true do you feel these words *I am in control,* on a scale of one to seven, where seven is completely true and one is completely false?

C: Five.

T: When you think about this difficult experience and the negative words, *I'm helpless,* what emotions do you feel now, when you think about this?

C: A certain prostration, as if my whole body were helpless, as if the helplessness were in my body. Until my body feels heavy, paralyzed. Helpless.

T: Helpless. On a scale of zero to ten, where zero means no distress and ten is the greatest distress that you can imagine, how much does it bother you now when you think about that now?

C: Ah, I have a seven.

T: Where do you feel that in your body?

C: Especially in my legs, as if my legs didn't have any strength.

T: As if they were paralyzed?

C: Paralyzed.

T: OK. So, go back and think about this difficult experience that you described and think about the negative words, *I'm helpless.*

Remember that you can always ask to stop. I'm going to do some movements, and we'll comment about what's going on between sets. Ready?

C: Ready.

T: So, go back and think about this difficult experience and think about the negative words, *I'm helpless*, feel this in your body and follow the movements. ([BLS} – in this case, the client asked for tactile movements on her hands.) Take a deep breath; let it out. What comes up?

C: No image came up. I only felt my leg becoming less tense.

T: Can we continue?

C: Sure

T: Go with that.

C: If I get some image am I supposed to tell you?

T: Yes, you can. [BLS]. Take a deep breath. What came up?

C: I have the image of my legs being really big and frozen, as if they were two blocks of ice.

T: Go with that. [BLS]. Take a deep breath. And now, what comes up?

C: Nothing; just a certain relief. No image.

T: Can we continue?

C: Yes.

T: OK. [BLS]. Take a deep breath. And now?

C: I don't know, I have a thought like this: I don't need to stay frozen for the rest of my life.

T: Think about that. [BLS].

C: I get the image… as if the chicken were there, and I give it a slap, and pull it off. Wow, this is crazy stuff! It's like a fury! I want to pick up this chicken and fly on top of it!

T: OK.

C: As if I were going to pick it up by the neck and squeeze it.

T: I understand.

C: And after I squeezed real hard on its neck, I could throw it aside and say, I'm not afraid of you anymore!

T: I understand.

C: I'm going to tell you what comes up. They are pretty disconnected. I see myself as a child, running, playing and saying, *I'm not going to worry about that chicken.*

T: Very well.

C: And suddenly, I'm a grown-up and the chicken is really little.

T: Wow!

C: It's just a chicken.

T: Yes. [BLS]. Take a deep breath. And now?

C: I don't know what's going on but I'm calmer.

T: Go back to that difficult experience, that you described, and on a scale of zero to ten, where ten is the greatest distress that you can imagine and zero is no distress, how much does it bother you now when you think about that?

C: Five.

T: What part still bothers you?

C: My grandmother. It showed up on my "inner" video, the image of my grandmother.

T: Go with that. [BLS].

C: My grandmother was a really mean person. She would keep saying: *there's not going to be enough food; there's not going to be enough money; your father is irresponsible.* The feeling of not having enough made me feel real frightened.

T: I understand.

C: She would always bad-mouth my father, and I didn't like to hear it. She would hide food, and then, just to provoke her, I would get it behind her back. When she found out, she would come after me. [Laughs] Something came to me: how long am I going to eat food just to provoke my grandmother?

T: That's right. How long?

C: Until I quit being silly. To show her that I can eat; that-she is dead and I'm still eating. Another thing that bothers me about her was making i look like my grandfather was the savior of the day, and that we were going to die of hunger, and needed to come up with food. It makes me angry, because I don't think anybody was dying of hunger there. It was more the feeling that there was going to be a lack, because no one ever really went hungry, it was just talk.

T: Go with that. [BLS].

C: I feel helpless when she talks like that. And I eat so I can show her I am powerful

T: Say again? (to emphasize what she had just said.).

C: I eat, not just to show her, because I would eat behind her back. I remember this stove. I can still see it. She would hide food there. On the top part there was a little drawer and I would go there and get what she had hidden there. I knew that what she had put there was for dinner and it was all counted out, but I got it anyway, even if I got spanked for. I would confront here. I would confront her anger.

T: Let's go with that. [BLS].

C: It was like I enjoyed attracting her anger towards me, and then I would be scared to death about it. Now the feeling in my leg is getting better.

T: Good.

C: The initial feeling in my leg was different than what it is now. Now it feels like my leg has bones, muscles, something that my foot can squeeze. The feeling is beginning to spread throughout all of my body, on my back. It's like a strength. It's like I can feel my body now. I have legs that can hold me up.

T: Say that again.

C: I see that I can stand on my own two legs. My legs don't need to be so heavy, that I can even run away if I need to so I don't get spanked all the time.

T: Go with that. [BLS].

C: I see the image of getting spanked a lot by my grandmother, with branches. There was a peach tree. She would cut some of those branches, and slap me on my legs. If I could, I would take away those branches from her hand. I would break then and throw them away, because that was a form of cowardice on her part. I was already going through so much living there. I didn't need that, too. It seems like the anger she had towards my dad got directed at me, because I would defend him. Every time she spoke ill of him, I would defend him. I'm getting a sense of freedom.

T: What that's like?

C: I don't understand. I can't explain it. It's as if I had been imprisoned in that part of the story. Now I see myself at seven years of age. All of a sudden I can leave that place, leave that part of my life behind because it was such torment.

T: [BLS]. Take a deep breath; one more time.

C: It's as if I could come out of my seven-year-old self.

T: Interesting.

C: And be my fifty-four years of age. At fifty-four I don't need to be afraid of my grandmother, the chickens, of going without food, of my grandfather having to bring us food. I can support myself.

T: That's right.

C: This gives support to my whole body. I always sit wrong. But now I feel myself sitting down.

T: I understand.

C: Like I'm on top of my legs, with my spine erect. That's how I would like to be. I can do this. I have been searching for this for a long time.

T: So, go back to that difficult experience we started with, on a scale of zero to ten, where ten is the greatest distress that you can imagine and zero is none, how much does it bother you now when you think about that?

C: Look, I got this picture: the first image was when I saw my grandfather coming and I would go running to him. But now, I see that I can stay where I am, there on the street where the house was, and just watch him come with his blue bag. I don't have to go running to him. With regard to the distress, I don't feel any. I can stay in place, but as an adult, just watching him come, knowing that he would never let there be any lack. That really moves me, knowing that there was a concerned adult. There was someone taking care of us, even though my mother was in bed and my father had disappeared; my grandmother was always picking a fight, but there was someone. And I see this picture of a door closing, as if I could say, *Enough. I want to close this door and open another one towards the future. Enough of this stuff.*

T: Great. It's like this tapping on m legs [The client had asked for the bilateral movements to be done on her legs] comes from my autonomy.

T: Yes.

C: Maybe this autonomy of not having to run to the blue bag, of being able to stand on my own feet.... This is so good! Very good! To know that I don't have to go running to the fridge and have my husband catch me at it in the middle of the night. [Laughs.] No danger. [Laughs].

T: Just so we can make one more assessment, on a scale of zero to ten, when you think about that difficult experience with which we started, how much does it bother you now?

C: No, nothing.

T: It's zero?

C: Zero.

T: Several expressions were mentioned as a positive cognition. You used the expression, *I'm in control*. Are these words still valid? So you want to reinforce these words or are there other positive words you prefer? During the session you said several other things like, *I am able, I can stand on my own legs.* You talked about autonomy, *I have autonomy. Of all of these expressions, which do you think is most appropriate?*

C: *I am able* is the best.

T: Is that what you want to reinforce?

C: I don't know what it is that I am able, but it feels the best. [Laughs]. Everything is OK.

T: Everything is OK, so, think about that initial experience.

C: Yes.

T: On a scale of one to seven, seven is completely true and one is completely false, how true do you feel the words are, *I am able*?

C: I am able.

T: Seven is true.

C: Seven. I feel a seven. It's incredible! The feeling in my legs is totally different. What happened? The body feeling is a seven, too.

T: Would you like to strengthen that a bit more?

C: Yes

T: Think about it. [BLS].

C: Something else came to me like, when I feel like attacking the fridge, will I really be able to do that? [Laughs].

T: Go with that. [BLS].

C: Something else came up: *I can choose.*

T: OK. On a scale of one to seven, how true do you feel are these words, *I can choose?*

C: I'll give it a six.

T: Give it a six?

C: Yes.

T: And what keeps it from being a seven?

C: Maybe I need to try it out.

T: I understand.

C: For real. In real life.

T: Think about this difficult experience with which we started, and the words, *I can choose,* and follow the movements.

C: Can I change the kind of movement?

T: Yes, of course.

C: I'd like to try eye movements.

T: OK, so think about these words, *I can choose,* and follow my fingers. ([BLS} Take a deep breath. And now?

C: It's comfortable.

T: Everything OK? On a scale of one to seven, seven is completely true and one is completely false.

C: Seven. I'm really comfortable.

T: Close your eyes for a moment. Think about that difficult experience with which we started, think about these positive words, *I can choose,* mentally examine your whole body, and tell me if you feel anything that bothers you.

C: It's interesting that now I feel it in my chest, but it's not a distress.

T: What do you feel in your chest?

C: It's like an expansion.

T: Let's strengthen that a bit more?

C: Yes.

T: Do you want eye movements or tapping?

C: You can snap your fingers close to my ears. [Client asks for auditory stimulation.]

T: I can do that, but just for a little while, ok? [Laughs]. Take a deep breath. Any distress?

C: The word that comes to me is *love*.

T: Think about that a little longer.

C: It's over.

T: It's really over.

C: Yes. It's really over. I don't need that anymore.

T: I don't need that anymore. Great! You know that the reprocessing we did today may continue after the session, so just take note of anything that comes up, so we can work on it in the future.

T: How are you now?

C: I'm good.

T: Your face looks a lot better

T: Great. Beautiful work, you did. Now, just out of curiosity… think about the chicken now.

C: It became so little! [Laughs]. I had thought about it! [Laughs]. Incredible! The image of the chicken… the first picture, it was really big, and then after I grabbed it by the neck, it became small. I threw it on the ground, and it just left. I said: *Fear, go away!* I don't know who this chicken is or what it represents to me.

T: But it's over, too!

C: Yes! It's over; it's over. Let's see how this works, that's why I gave it a six!

T: Good.

C: Chicken and fridges, let's see. [Laughs] But you know, it's a *let's see*, almost as if it were a certainty.

T: Well, you'll have to tell us later on!

C: Yes, I'll tell you. [Laughs].

T: Just great! Thank you so much!

Resilience

Some years later, I did another session with Mary Francis. When we met again she had lost more than 35 pounds! She was elegant and happy. No longer did she transmit that picture of sadness and depression from the first session. She didn't even remember that she had been afraid of chickens! She wanted to work on something else.

One of the things we look for in EMDR therapy is the touchstone event: the first experience that became the trigger for subsequent symptoms. That is why we ask clients to think about the other times in their lives that they felt or thought the same way they are thinking or feeling now. It is always incredible and surprising to see the kinds of memories that come up.

This session with Mary Francis is especially touching when we consider the family limitations with which she struggled as a child. We see what the impact that the love and appreciation of *one person* can make in the life of someone else. Four years of unselfish emotional investment through the channel of sewing classes brought routine and stability into Mary Francis' life. Perhaps it totally changed the direction of her life. Let's let her tell her story:

C: It's hard to focus on a phrase that I would like to work on today. It's a feeling of not being able to do a good job with my professional activities. I think I work too much and earn too little. At the same time, I hear people say that they see the same number of clients, and I think, *how come they can do it and I can't? If my office is full of clients, like everybody would want theirs to be... What am I going to do with all of this? How could I send anyone away?* It's a conflict. I'm living a conflict that is even hurting my health situation.

T: In what way?

C: In what way? [Laughs.] I have this indisposition in my stomach. Almost every day when I finish working, I feel this thing. It's a really big indisposition. It has a little bit to do with the issue of food, that we worked on the last time. It's like I still need to have food in order to relax.

119

T: So, when you think your work and the words you mentioned: *I'm being exploited; I'm not able; my workload is too heavy,* go back a little bit in your past, look over your memories, and see when you felt this way before. Maybe it was some time in your childhood or adolescence. [Patient is quiet for a few moments while she thinks.}

C: Yes, it's something that feels clear in my adolescence.

T: When you go back to…

C: I was about twelve years old. My father never liked working. He never held down a steady job. He always did the odd job, a crazy life, so there was a lot of lack of money at home. I remember I didn't have very many clothes. The first time I want to meet with a boyfriend, I wore my mother's dress. Once I visited New York, because my father's family was from there. Now, my father's family was rich, but my dad was the black sheep. He was always the black sheep of the family. He raised four kids without working, just hanging on to this crazy life. So I went to visit a girlfriend with my grandmother's dress. Today I think about how ridiculous that must have been.

So when I was twelve, I started learning to sew. I went to classes because I wanted to have clothes to wear. I remember once at the beginning of my adolescence, I must have been about eleven, and a paternal aunt said: *we come to the beach with these children, but they don't have anything to wear!* I was ashamed of that. So I decided to take sewing classes, but my mother was very rigid. The condition she imposed to pay for the classes was that I had to sew for the whole family. That made me very angry. I spent years in sewing classes, and I had to sew for us, so we could go to parties, my sister and I. My sister got all of her clothing ready! I remember crying at sewing classes, on top of the table, because the day of the party was arriving and I still had to make my dress and my sister's! The teacher would feel sorry for me and would help me. This weight comes from back then. If I didn't do it, no one did, and it just wouldn't happen.

T: If we were to choose a photograph of this situation, what would it look like?

C: I see myself on the sewing table crying. I was desperate. The party was on Saturday, and it was Thursday, and I just wasn't going to be able to finish it all. And if I didn't finish, I knew my mother wouldn't let me go to the prom. Plus I had to make my dress and my sister's. I can still see it.

When I was fifteen, my mother bought this really, really cheap cloth for me and my sister. It was for our debutante dresses. I hated it that I had to make her dress, too! I would get mad every time I had to work on her dress, because I wanted to work on mine, but, no. I had to make both of them.

T: When you think about this difficult experience, what words best describe what you think about yourself now, that are negative, false and irrational?

C: That it takes a lot of effort for me to do things. I also think, I'm not going to be able to do it. Both of those things: it's too heavy, and I won't be able to do it.

T: Could it be, *I am exploited*?

C: When I had to make a shirt for my brother, I really hated it! When I had to make the buttonholes...! And I love to sew, OK? I remember making those first dresses for my daughter with enormous pleasure, but no one made me do that. That's what I would like to feel about my work. That I didn't have to feel obliged by it. My husband and I faced a recent financial loss, fairly significant, and that really did something with me about working at my office.

T: I have to work.

C: *I have to work.*

T: I am obliged to work.

C: *I'm incapable*, because he [husband] doesn't have it.

T: So, which is the best expression? I'm not capable?

C: I think so. It's the strongest one

T: Strongest?

C: Because it gets me in my stomach.

T: So that's what gets you in your stomach: I'm not capable?

C: Yes. In order to be capable of doing it, I have to eat [Laughs].

T: You have to have lots of energy?

C: Lots of energy.

T: Now when you think about difficult situation, what words best describe what you would like to think about yourself that are positive?

C: That I can do things with pleasure.

T: I do things with pleasure?

C: *I do it with pleasure*. Without feeling exploited, but because I want to do it.

T: When you think about this difficult experience, on a scale of one to seven, where seven is completely true and one is completely false, how true do you feel these positive words, *I do it with pleasure,* are now?

C: Three.

T: And when you think about this difficult experience and the negative words, *I'm incapable*, what emotions come up for you now?

C: Sometimes, It's despair, because I fell like I'm in a dead-end street. I have to do it and there's no way out. I am stuck. There is no way out. It's a real despair.

T: And when you think about this difficult experience, how much does it bother you now, on a scale of zero to ten, where ten is the greatest distress and zero is none?

C: Right now, it's not real high, but when I am inside of it all, it's a ten.

T: How high is it now?

C: Now? A seven.

T: Where do you feel it in your body?

C: In my stomach.

T: Mary Francis, we're going to start our processing. This isn't the first time you do EMDR. You know how it works. You have your safe, calm place in case you need it. And you can always ask to stop, if necessary.

Go back and think about that difficult experience you were describing to me. Think about the negative words *I'm incapable,* see where you feel this in your body and follow the movements. (BLS.)

C: Two things come to me. First: it is not fair to make a child do this! Second: some of those things were really too difficult for my age. For example, making buttonholes was really hard for me. I can see myself going to the sewing machine, trying to do those blessed buttonholes. ([BLS}.)

C: This reprocessing went on longer. I saw a lot of things. I remember the voice of the teacher. She was Japanese, and I can remember her exact tone, yelling at the boys and what she would say. I remember her speaking Japanese. There were other adolescents. I remember the laughter we shared. And I realized, wow! Those years I spent there that seemed so terrible, really had a lot of good things about them. I must have spent three or four years there. What came to me was, Mrs. Smith was so good to me. She really liked me. Sometimes I stayed after class, when everyone had already left, and she would do what my mother never did. [Mary Frencis cries.] She would help me, because my mother always pushed the problems onto me. But she never taught me what to do with the problems. With Mrs. Smith, it was different. She not only helped me, she would teach me how to do it. I never realized how important a person she was! And I was a handful! Four years... and I never gave up.

T: Perseverant...

C: My mother was a very depressed person. She helped me very little. My mother counted on my help, but I could never count on her. A few years later, when I was about fifteen, my mother got so depressed I had to bathe her. That was very unpleasant. But in a way, Mrs. Smith gave me what I didn't have at home. I didn't just learn to sew. It was those afternoons there with her. [Silence while Mary Francis thinks about that.]

T: Now go back and think about all of this. On a scale of zero to ten, where ten is the maximum and zero is none, how much does it bother you now?

C: Five.

T: What is this five?

C: What is this five? It's that lack of having been cared for, you know? The lack of a father that could give me a dress when I needed one; of not having had a mother who could teach me stuff, instead of expecting it out of me. My parents, my house… it was all very chaotic. However, I managed to come out whole from all of that. I had some resilience! I know that. But I think I have traces of having survived all of that. My mother was esquizophrenic. She wasn't able to deal with life because it was really difficult at home. I'm the only one who really made it in life, even with all of those difficulties. But there are places inside of me that are not filled up: a lack of significant adults, that would give me what I needed, that would teach me how to do things. I never had people that I could count on like that.

T: But you found out you had Mrs. Smith.

C: Yes, I had Mrs. Smith. I had Mrs. Smith.

T: And today you have yourself.

C: It's as if inside of me there were still these holes. It's the lack of care. I had to build my life as best I could. But I never gave up! But every once in a while, they show up. When they do, I get the feeling, *I'm incapable* or *I'm being exploited.* I had to start working very early. There were some advantages with that. I started working when I was only sixteen. I gave private lessons. I was able to retire early, and study Psychology. So I had these advantages, but I still have these holes inside of my stomach. They're places where I lack structure.

T: I guess that in a way we could say that here we are talking with two people. One is a twelve-year-old girl and the other is you, the adult. And you have these holes. How about you visit thee holes and see what you can do about it?

C: Wow! That would be great! For years I've wanted to do that!

T: Let's do it?

C: Yes. How do you want me to do it?

T: Think about it for a little bit.

C: Now you really got me. I don't even know where to begin.

T: Let's make an attempt, and if you have any difficulty, we'll help you. [BLS].

C: The picture that came to me was one of a well.

T: I see.

C: Me, looking inside this well. This well was in a house I where I once lived. I used to take water out of it.

T: I see.

C: The water would come out really clean. I thought, *it may be a deep well, but we take good water out of it*. And then I saw one of those irons that we used to use, that had live coals in it, so we could iron our clothing. It was a cool place – I loved this house. It was a place of refuge to where I could run. In the middle of a field there was a big log. I used to balance on top of it. So, in the midst of so much junk, I always managed to find something good for me.

T: Fantastic.

C: I would run away. I would go to this place and no one could find me.

T: *"But I was always able to find good things for myself"*.

C: I think so! [Laughs]. So two things come to me: this phrase, *I can find good things for myself,* and also…*she was good to me.*

T: Right.

C: I think that's it. I think of my dad, and I think of my husband. He was something really good that I found for myself.

T: Yes.

C: So was my grandfather. Today I see that I found a husband who had a lot of the same characteristics as my grandfather, somebody who takes cares of others.

T: Yes.

C: There were two times when I went against my dad, because he was very important to me, so I never crossed him. The first time was when I wanted to go to work. He had that rich family mentality, vain and uppity. He wouldn't help me. He would help at home, but he was all-uppity. A schoolteacher asked me to tutor her son. She was from a foreign country and the children had difficulty in learning the language. I went to tutor the young boy and my dada said, *You're not going to be anybody's babysitter. No daughter of mine is going to take care of other people's kids.* And I replied: *Yes I am! Because you don't buy shoes for me and I need to have nice things.* I don't know where I found do much courage, because I was never brave about saying things to him.

Then, when I met my husband he said: *This guy is worthless. You can't marry this guy.* But there was never a doubt in my mind that he was The One, and that I was going to marry him no matter what my father said. I knew that he was something good for me. That really moves me [Cries] in a very special way. From somewhere inside of me I found the resources to build good things for myself. My marriage had its difficult moments, but I always thought like this: *this marriage is going to get good.* So I sought out couple therapy, and today we have a really solid marriage, very solid. Even though my husband has his issues with his family of origin, we have solid children. So we were able to find good things! Build good things together! [Laughs] Even if he were a rock tyrant, we fought side by side.

T: So, let's go back to that difficult experience; on a scale of zero to ten, what's it like now? Ten is the maximum of distress and zero is none.

C: Wow! I get something like, that weight was like a huge stone. When I look at my life, and think of all of the good things that have come out of my life... it's like each side of a set of scales. I don't know how to explain it. The stone on one side and the good things on the other side. I don't have to keep looking at the stone any longer. The truth is, I would like to only look at the good things! [Laughs]. And I think of something like this: *if life is so light, why do I need to eat so much?* [Laughs]. It's a matter of building a lighter future. That's what I have been saying to my husband: that I would like to age in a healthy manner, lighter, without having to kill ourselves.

T: Go back to that initial scene. Now on a scale of zero to ten, where ten is the greatest distress and zero is none, how much does it bother you now?

C: Go back to that scene?

T: Right.

C: Wow! The scene is far away. As if it had gone into a time tunnel. Now I think it's zero.

T: Let me ask you something. You said you had holes of lack of having been cared for.

C: Yes, I do.

T: You do now?

C: Maybe I need to change more of my beliefs then. It's that I was raised with a kind of omnipotence that I care for myself, because my father was useless. My mother was also incapable. I took care of myself. My father couldn't do it; neither could my mother. But the truth is, it wasn't me that took care of me. It was God who put people in my life who did it. My grandfather was a very important person. And then there was Mrs. Smith. I met other people during my lifetime that fulfilled the roles that my parents couldn't. They were really disturbed. And then there is my husband who does that for me to this day. Some days, when I come home and start complaining, he makes pizza or something. Maybe he could learn to make something "lighter", right? [Laughs].

T: Tell him, *let's change the menu?* [Laughs]

C: So, as you can see, there were many people who took care of me, not just my mom or dad, but others.

T: But...? [BLS]

C: There's still something there. It's like I can see those people. And I see a picture like a newspaper, where some things are written, but there's also white space. And these empty places were being written in.

I remember a picture of when I was in first grade, and my grandmother would draw things on my notebooks. I really wanted my mother to have done that, but she was always sick. Then I saw a picture of my mom. She was standing next to my grandmother who had the notebook. I wanted to color the newspaper, but there wasn't enough time, because you stopped the movements. [Laughs] [BLS]

Ever since I was a child, one of the really great things I learned from my mother and grandmother was this thing about religiosity. The image of the newspaper changed to a book written in gold, as if it were the book of my life. There's a part where I feel like God is talking to me. I have never been alone. God has always

127

provided. The experience of faith and spirituality is something I always grabbed on to during my most difficult moments. I learned that with my mother. Before I came here, I said this to her: *I have a purpose. Look, I need prayer, because things are too heavy for me right now.*

T: I'm not sure I understand?

C: Even with all her lack of structure, stuff she just couldn't give me, she gave me this strength, the ability to pull water out of wells.

T: Yes.

C: To really be able to close up the holes. Today I am 56 years old, and if I could, I would redeem this! Incredible. Fantastic, really fantastic.

T: So go back and think about that situation when you were a child, and see if these words are still valid. You mentioned other things as well. I will repeat them and you tell me which most resonates with you. You started saying, *"what I do with pleasure"*, but you also said, *"I can pull water out of wells"*, *"I am capable"*, *"I can do this"*.

C: I think the belief is the basic one: *"I'm not capable"* and *"I can do it"*, *"I am capable"*.

T: Which is better?

C: Funny, in my head it's like the verb wants to change to, I did it, I made it, as if it was a done thing.

T: So if I did it, I can fill in the holes?

C: Yes, of course.

T: So think about that experience, and think about those words. [BLS]

C: Funny, I see this picture: that little girl, bent over, as if she were looking at the future, to life, not knowing if she will make it. It's as if I can look backwards and say to her, *I made it*.

T: So, let's do that. Bring the little girl here, and I would like for ou to talk to her. What is it she needs? She needs to hear it from you. [BLS].

C: Yes, if I had to say something to her, it would be like: *you are capable because you have resources. And God is with you, and you have lots of people.*

T: Use your imagination.

C: Go to that scene?

T: Go to that scene and say those things to the little girl who is 12.

C: OK. [BLS]. Something really interesting came up. It's like this: you can do it. You can do it with pleasure. And when you can do it with pleasure, it takes away the anxiety. Because I got it done, but I always had this feeling that I wasn't capable. The anxiety was always very present and so I had very little pleasure in it. So, if I can do what I like, if I can do it with pleasure, then I can do it without anxiety. So, that puts an end to it

T: One more little thing. Go back there and talk to that little girl. Ask her if she can now do things with pleasure, without anxiety, and without feeling exploited. [BLS].

C: Yes, because deep down she wanted to please her father and mother when she made all of that clothing. You could say: *she made it for me,* since my sister would have a fit and just not do it.

T: Your sister didn't learn how to sew.

C: You know what my sister says? The one who's nuts? Sometimes I say, *it must be nice to be crazy!* [Laughs] She says, "*The Universe gives me everything I need*". So, one day, I had a fight with her, and I said: *The Universe has a name and an address, right? Here at home! Of course it gives you everything you need!* But there were times when I was really envious and would think, *why didn't I turn out like her, and let the Universe do it for me.*

T: Why didn't you turn out like her?

C: [Laughs] Because I chose differently. But I can choose to stay in the middle. I don't want to stay on the opposite end either. I can choose to stay in the middle.

T: Very well, just great. Ask your little twelve-year-old little girl if she can do things without feeling exploited, do them with pleasure, without anxiety. See if she can do that. [BLS].

C: Her reply is: *I have to do things more slowly, calmly.*

129

T: So let's work that out with her?

C: Instead of making so many clothes, make fewer, ok! The phrase that comes to me, *I can do less.*

T: I can do less. I can make things just for me. I can make things for my sister when I feel like it. I can make things for others, if I want to, because now, *I can choose.*

C: Yes, but I said, *It's hard.* I can choose. You know something? I need to choose something. I need to quit being stupid, and charge more for my sessions; and choose to work less.

T: I would feel less exploited. I'm still kind of stupid about that.

T: The feeling I have is that the other child, the one you have acquired now, the positive one, is the one that says: *I can choose; I can chose what I do; I can choose how much I charge; I can choose how many hours a week I am going to work.*

C: Yes. I can choose to see more children and adolescents which I just love, and fewer adults. I think that's something I want for now: working less with adults and do more child therapy.

T: OK, so now when you think about these words, *I can do it,* are these the words you would like to reinforce? Or would you prefer, *I can choose?*

C: This "capable" also includes being able to choose.

T: OK. Capable of choosing, then. Great. On a scale of one to seven, seven is completely true and one is false, how true do you feel these words to be, *I am capable?*

C: I'm still a little afraid of not being able to do it, but it's just a little bit now; not much.

T: And where is this little bit of fear?

C: I get the feeling that if I charge more, my patients will all go away.

T: So, maybe you will have to choose how you want to do things? Think about it, reevaluate, re-accomodate, things like that. Go back to the little girl. How is she?

C: Fine.

T: How are these words, *I am capable,* on a scale of one to seven?

130

C: Seven.

T: Powerful seven?

C: Look here, a powerful seven. Just think, back then if I had chosen not to make things for my sister, my mother would have pulled me out of the sewing course.

T: And you would have lost Mrs. Smith.

C: And I wouldn't have had any clothes.

T: And you wouldn't have had any clothes.

C: That's what transfers to the office today. I get it! If I decide that, *I am capable*, and raise my prices, I just have to run that risk.

T: Perhaps you will lose a few patients in the beginning, and acquire news ones later?

OK, let's do a body scan. How is everything?

C: Fine.

T: Everything OK?

C: Yes, just fine.

T: You know that the processing may continue after the session is over.

C: [Laughs] Great!

T: I think there are things that will still re-accommodate inside. You have some challenges ahead of you, but I would like to say how much I admire you. This resilience you've had. And it seems that you weren't as orphaned as you thought. So many people came into your life and cared for you.

I also thought about how the sewing course was an oasis in your life that nurtured you. It gave you some really good things. Your sister never received that. She lost the stability, the routine, that predictability that the sewing course – and Mrs. Smith – brought into your life.

C: Sewing course... now I sew people! [Laughs]

T: Isn't that wonderful! You didn't have choices back then, but now you can choose how you want to deal with your work.

C: Wow! I am very capable! Just great!

T: I feel privileged to have accompanied you in this process.

C: I am really happy! You are the one who installed my safe

131

place. Today I think things came together in a way I never expected.

T: My only recommendation is that you continue to care for the little twelve-year-old inside of you. Take her with you. Let her know that you are taking care of her, protecting her. Now she has a "mother" who can take care of her.

C: Thank you.

Next day:
We did a quick evaluation session the next day.

T: I'd like to know how you are doing today and if anything happened between yesterday and today?

C: I'm fine. What I perceived from yesterday is a slowing down of my inner rhythm.

T: How interesting.

C: There was a moment when I was talking to my grandmother, and it seemed that I was in slow motion. [Laughs]. Because I am more the agitated type. I saw myself talking to her and thought: *wow, I'm in slow motion*

T: Do you think that is a good thing?

C: Yes.

T: Are you calmer now?

C: Yes, I am.

T: Are you seeing things with greater tranquility?

C: Yes, I need this.

T: I agree. Did you dream anything?

C: I don't remember any dreams. I just went to bed early and slept like a rock.

T: Did you sleep well?

C: Very well.

T: OK, let's go back to the scene where the little girl is at the sewing machine. When you think about that, is anything different?

C: Just the same thing I told you yesterday: it's just far away.

T: And when you think about this, on a scale of zero to ten, where ten is the greatest distress and zero is none, how much does it bother you now when you think about this?

C: Zero.

T: And what did you learn with that session?

C: Wow, just a lot of things!

T: How about two or three? OR do you want to keep it to yourself?

C: Today, when I was coming here, I caught myself thinking, my life is so rich! I was saying my prayers and thinking about the richness of my life. Another thing that I think I need to continue to reprocess is that I don't need to fill these holes; because every time I felt myself in one of them I would have one of my eating attacks. I don't know how things are going to turn out, but I'm beginning to believe that I'm not going to have to fill the holes with food.

T: There are other solutions? Or no need to fill them?

C: I don't need to fill them. Now it's a matter of having a conversation with my body and making amends with it for all of the wrong things that I did to myself. When I got really desperate I put all sorts of things inside, trying to fill up the holes.

T: If we had more time, Mary Francis, I would offer to work on how we could help you fill up the holes and how you would like to accommodate these things inside, how you would make amends with your body. Since we don't have the time today, it will have to be seen in another session. What really makes me happy are the results from yesterday. Today you look wonderful!

C: And no holes! [Laughs].

T: And no holes.

C: Without the sensation of the holes. This thing about eating… I don't know if I have to work on it. I think it's something I need to do with myself, a conversation I need to have with myself. I didn't have time to do it yesterday, because I wanted to rest. But I feel that it's part of the process of closing things down and that it will happen naturally.

T: So, once again, I'd like to thank you for letting us accompany you in this process.

C: It was my privilege.

T: It has been an opportunity to see a bit of your life, and how you have become an overcomer.

C: Thank you.

Several years later, I sought out Mary Francis to ask for permission to include her story in this book. She authorized it and wrote:

It was very nice to read these sessions. I perceive how different my life is today. I don't feel exploited by anyone anymore.

Four years ago we moved to the capital city. My husband had a heart attack and I stopped working for a few months to care for him. That's when my first grandson was born, and I got involved with two more grandchildren that were born soon afterwards. Family life has involved me in such a pleasant way that I kept postponing my return to work.

Now I see that even to let go of working an inner healing is necessary. I don't reproach myself for not earning so much money. I have a small retirement stipend as a schoolteacher, and that is enough. I don't have to "be capable". I can stay home and enjoy my family, or travel, or do patchwork, which is something I love. It's a place where I meet wonderful women with whom I laugh and talk. After all, sewing is a great pleasure in m life because it taught me how to bring together and match the rich patches of life. Thank you.

More books by TraumaClinic Edições

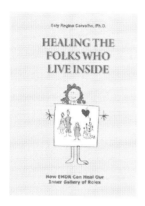

For more information on this book or to purchase a copy, please visit our e-store:

Healing the Folks Who Live Inside
https://www.createspace.com/4229106

For more information on this book or to purchase a copy, please visit our e-store:

Heal Your Brain: Heal Your Body
https://www.createspace.com/5692056

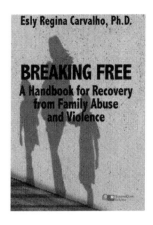

For more information on this book or to purchase a copy, please visit our e-store:

Breaking Free
https://www.createspace.com/5310779

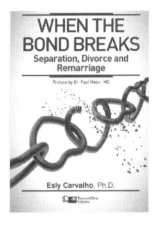

For more information on this book or to purchase a copy, please visit our e-store:

When the Bond Breaks
https://www.createspace.com/4956447

For more information visit: www.plazacounselingservices.com

If you would like to sign up to receive our newsletter about events and publications visit the following link:
https://app.e2ma.net/app2/audience/signup/1773350/1732906/?v=a

Printed in Great Britain
by Amazon